10
PRINCIPLES
to a
LIVING
SPIRITUALITY

HOW TO DISCOVER
THE ESSENCE
OF LOVE

JAKOB MERCHANT

Designed by Andrej Rudolf Semnic
Editor: Kim Catanzarite
Format/Layout:
ISBN-10: 1-950874-00-1
ISBN-13: 978-1-950874-00-2

Stay in touch with Rev. Jakob

Find details about his services and how to join his email lists

at

www.jakobmerchant.com

Communion with Love Publishing

www.communionwithlove.com

Contact us directly

at

info@communionwithlove.com

Find a full list of services and offerings in the appendix at the back
of the book

Love is All,

Love is All That Exists.

In praise of 10 Principles to a Living Spirituality and Rev. Jakob's work

Jakob is the purest manifestation of Love I have been blessed to spend time with in this lifetime. Through grace, I have traveled a lot all over the world, have met countless people in many areas of life, and if I had to name the one who is radiating forth the purest lovingness it would be Jakob.

We met over ten years ago and since then I have witnessed his way very closely. He came to the United States with literally nothing, "just" having along his most pure intention of being a servant to God and his fellow men. I saw all that is present today evolving miraculously out of nothing, workshops and retreats, Communion with Love with all his wonderful activities or the Surrender-Retreat-House in Sedona. It all has manifested only by the Grace of Divinity due to Jakob's purest intention of being in selfless service to God's will.

I have attended many workshops and retreats with him, and we are still in contact on a regular basis since our first encounter. With deep humility and gratitude, I can state:

His loving Presence and his profound knowledge about Divinity in all its expressions are important reasons why I transformed into a totally different person than the one I had been the first time we met. But the most wonderful impact of it is that due to this profound and loving internal transformation, I am able to help many people in my life today.

In my personal experience and by all what I have witnessed over the years, I can say from the bottom of my heart Jakob IS the Radiance of Divine Love that is healing and transformative for those coming in contact with him. Jakob is my living example of selfless and loving service to God's will and my fellow men.

Peter Schaefer
June 10, 2019
Asbach, Germany

Experiences with Rev. Jakob's Work

"Only someone who is rooted and lives his life in Divinity and Love can bring such teachings to all. I consider Rev. Jakob to be an example of that Love and one whose life has become his teachings. Rev. Jakob is truly gifted in his teachings and healing techniques, and I am very blessed and grateful to have come across his work"–[CHETAN AMALEAN OF CHARLOTTE, NORTH CAROLINA]

"Infinite Grace through this man's work supports my evolution of Consciousness; you need to let him support yours."–[ROMY ALEXANDRA OF SEDONA, ARIZONA]

"I am incredibly fortunate and grateful to have known and worked with Jakob Merchant. In my work with him, the age-old question of how to translate spiritual teachings and knowledge into experiential reality has begun to be realized, and my experience of Love, Joy, and Peace has deepened significantly. The boogeymen of depression, anxiety, fear, and shame used to be relegated to a dark corner within myself to be cursed at and distracted from. Jakob has shown me not only how to heal and grow from them but to utilize them as avenues to sustainable spiritual growth. Having been exposed to many spiritual pathways, groups, and teachers, and the pitfalls inherent in the spiritual community, I tend toward caution when hearing about new spiritual teachers that are held in high esteem. With Jakob, I place deep trust in this regard, and have experienced him to be a legitimate spiritual teacher on the pathway of Ultimate Truth and Love. My greatest wish for any friend or family member would be for them to experience the Love available in this pathway. It is my hope that many others are blessed to do so. "–[RYAN MCGINTY OF SEDONA, ARIZONA]

"Jakob is profoundly dedicated to helping others experience the Love that is already present within us. His guided meditations, devotional services, prayers, and courses come right from the heart. The Love there is unmistakable!"–[SUSAN ADAMS OF SEDONA, ARIZONA]

Dedication

Grace manifests as all that exists.
This Grace of Love has brought forth this book.

JAKOB MERCHANT

Special thanks to the following people:

Fabiola Merchant
Analiz, Amber, and Angeleah Merchant
Francis Merchant
Dr. David R. Hawkins and Susan Hawkins
Ibrahim and Marianne Merchant
Chetan Amalean, Romy Alexandra, Jenine Gobbi,
Virginia Schlitt, Jonathan Mann
Susan and Kriya Adams
Steven Clough
Diane Berke and Jeffrey K. Zeig
Paul Bullock
Every single being

Love Guarantee

Rev. Jakob believes that there is nothing more important than you feeling loved in everything he does. Therefore, if you're not happy or satisfied, he will offer a 100 percent refund. This offer also applies to this book. If you would like to return this book, contact us at the following email address: **info@communionwithlove.com**. Please provide your receipt. We will refund your money after we receive the book.

Help us to improve the work. Send us an email with any questions or suggestions for improvement. You may also join our mailing list dedicated to improving the work. Contact us via email to sign up. You will receive book manuscripts or workshop and course outlines several times a year to review.

Foreword by Timothy Conway

Rev. Jakob and his family exude gentleness, kindness and love. This book, apparently little in size, points back to the vastness of who and what we truly are – Divine LOVE. This is the great God Reality, the source of our lives, the very substance of our being, the awesome power by which we move, speak, listen, think, feel and sense and without this power we are literally nothing.

In these pages, you can read Jakob's distillation of ten timeless spiritual principles about how to turn the selfish life over to the infinite-eternal life of the God-Self and thereby dissolve limited identity into boundless LOVE, and truly live this LOVE with the great virtues of humility, integrity, and all other qualities and capacities of authentic sages, saints and living buddhas.

Jakob has also shared some background about his own spiritual journey and provided ways for the reader to go beyond reading, reflecting and integrating, even though this may be entirely sufficient for many spiritual aspirants. The book then shows ways of staying in touch with Jakob in deeper healing modalities. These include spiritual counseling, courses and workshops, online events, surrender retreats, the Health & Healing Clinic, and staying at the Merchants' lovely Sedona Surrender Retreat House which is located very close to some world-famous scenic locations. Truly, LOVE is our Truth, the great Divine Reality doing everything and being everyone. We are always the singularity of LOVE somehow non-dually dancing and delighting in relationship as LOVER and BELOVED. Let this book be a portal on the pathless journey from here to HERE... the immensity and intimacy of LOVE.

Timothy Conway of Peoria, Arizona

Foreword by Shifu Giuseppe Medlin

This small but mighty book carries such a pure level of devotion and faith that you can't help but become inspired to revive your own unique connection to God. It is rare to find such a person who can walk the spiritual path and be able to communicate eloquently the depth of the wisdom gained. There is an honoring of God and sharing that a life filled with love is what success is in this life and to be surrendered to love is our highest ideal of awakening. He has creatively awakened the teaching of "*Through God all things are possible*" by sharing the experience of how love is needed to awaken oneself. I enjoyed feeling the pure vein of love and devotion that this book emanated, and while reading I could feel the inspirational faith behind the words. There is nothing empty about this book; it is filled with decadent spiritual food that will leave you feeling fulfilled mentally, emotionally, and spiritually. I would recommend this book and all the teachings to anyone on the spiritual path, from those just starting their journey to well-seasoned spiritual aspirants.

Blessings,
Shifu Giuseppe Medlin of Sedona, Arizona

JAKOB MERCHANT

Letter to The Reader

To the reader,

My life is dedicated to helping you live a life that is alive, inspired, and centered as Love, surrender, and illumination. Everything manifests as the Grace of Love; the fact that you are holding this book in your hands is due to God's love for you. This moment is his calling to your evolution. You may have gone to many places and experienced many things. Being led to this book is the invitation to go on a new but familiar journey—the journey of returning back home.

My life's purpose is to not only be that state of spirituality described in this book but also to be a guide for those who choose to be the Light, be the Love, be a living spirituality.

It is my hope that my purpose and yours will intersect by journeying together throughout this book and beyond.

I love you.

How to Use This Book

This book is designed so that one is able to read it in a short period of time and subsequently use it for a lifetime. The concepts presented are purposefully short and precise so that the "I"'s defense mechanism in response to excessive information can be bypassed. Instead of amassing vast amounts of spiritual information, the invitation is to make the information presented in this book come alive. Studying, practicing, and living any of these spiritual principles will facilitate a monumental effect on one's spirituality.

These principles are not new; they have been well established throughout history. What makes them new is the emphasis put on them and lack of distraction surrounding them, so that they are in the spotlight of the Spirit. Because these principles deserve continuous attention, time, and energy, this book can be read an infinite number of times, and each time will deepen the direct experience of each principle.

One can also focus on one page per day, per week, per month, or even per year, and thereby deepen each quality, making it what one is. Each chapter includes an "invitation" for meditation and contemplation. This book is a companion book to the online course 10 Days to a Living Spirituality. Here it serves as an introduction to each lesson and guided meditation.

This book is intended to be carried in day-to-day life so that in any given situation it can be opened and the solution to any problem, spiritual or otherwise, can be found.

This book is designed to be a reminder, a focusing tool for the components of a living spirituality.

JAKOB MERCHANT

Introduction

Everyone has had a moment where they wished their spirituality was more alive. Not just in rare and special occasions but day to day, moment to moment. A living spirituality is where one's life is enlivened by spirituality at all times and in all circumstances. This permanent spirituality is the promise of living spirituality, and this book, 10 Principles to a Living Spirituality, is the distillation and essence of that.

If you were stranded on a deserted island called "your life," and you could only bring one book to meet all your spiritual needs, this is the book you would take.

Every generation faces unique challenges. One of the challenges of this current generation is that the essence of the direction for a spiritual life has been buried in a vast amount of information available. The problem is not finding spiritual information; rather the problem is now how to discern what is real and important, and to make it applicable in one's life. While there are countless books on religion and spirituality, 10 Principles to a Living Spirituality provides readers with a short, precise, and, complete spirituality. The book and its inherent spirituality can not only be carried everywhere, but is all that one needs on one's life's journey.

The main body of the book contains ten principles that are critical for one's spiritual evolution. Without the application of these qualities, spirituality cannot exist. The book will open with a summary and vision of the integration of a living spirituality uniting all principles into one integrated spirituality. This vision of the one thing one needs to know is the summary of everything that is offered in all spiritual Truth.

In addition, the book covers humility, intention, prayer, consistency and unconditional practice, the personal will, Love, surrender to Love, the I's identifications, integrity, and spiritual practices and routines.

The appendix provides further information and resources on where to find more support and help on the spiritual journey as well as a deepening of the topics in this book.

JAKOB MERCHANT

Preface

I remember lying in bed in my small room in Austria. The room was empty, and it was silent. The sun was filling the air itself with warmth, and life was going on somewhere, but not here. Everything stood still. In fact, it was so still that the stillness not only filled the room but filled me from the inside. Then this silence was filled by an inner Light. This Light within me, within Consciousness, began more and more to fill me and became more present while my room and everything in it—the walls, the bed, and even my body—faded away. I began to experience that Light, which was only Love, as the only thing that existed: no time, no world, no thoughts. Only conscious awareness of Light and Love.

These experiences followed me throughout my childhood. For most of my life, I did not think of it or talk about it; I wished and longed, however, to have someone to guide me through these experiences.

My childhood was filled with tremendous Love and joy. I was drawn to philosophy, psychology, and spirituality from an early age. Many questions around Love surfaced over the years and spiritual experiences began to occur. I wished I had a guide to not only explain these happenings to me, but more importantly, to help me make spirituality permanently alive in my life.

Decades later, with the help of numerous teachers, teachings, and most significantly, life experiences, it became clear what the ultimate human endeavor is—the journey through one's life as a spiritual experience. Life itself is the spiritual experience that one is seeking; the means to provide that is the promise of living spirituality.

Whether this book can benefit the reader is answered by the spirituality and Love one experiences in one's life. One knows when one is complete because the Love that is present is so complete that one merely wants to dissolve into it and allow that Love to be all that is.

May this book lead everyone to that Love, a permanent spirituality.

Rev. Jakob Merchant
March 22, 2019

Table of Contents

11. Appendix and Further Resources

1

PRINCIPLE

The One Thing You Need to Know

INVITATION[1]

Love is all, Love is all that exists

Love is all, Love is all that exists. This Love radiates forth as all of manifestation. There is no individual, and with that, there is no individual self that has the power to cause events to occur in the world, such as moving a body, speaking, or thinking thoughts. Everything within form is an autonomous unfoldment of the creation of Love.

With that understanding, the illusionary "I" can surrender to Love, dissolve into that Love, and allow for the Glory of Love to unfold. Nothing further is needed to realize the ultimate reality.

---

1 The invitations in each chapter are meant to be meditated and contemplated on.

One Living Spirituality

All spiritual progress is a progressional deepening of the experience of Love. Love replaces the illusions of the "I" and its expressions, such as the mind, thoughts, and mentalization[2] , positions taken about anything and everything, and most importantly the dream of an "I" separate from Love.

The spiritual qualities outlined in these ten principles build upon each other and synergistically deepen that experience of Love. Out of radical humility arises devotional Love and the intention to give one's self to that Love. This is facilitated via the process of continuous intention as well as spiritual practice. Intention is what spiritualizes any moment and allows a person to become one with Love via surrender to Love. Giving one's life to Love in every moment frees one from the world of form as one becomes the infinite out of which everything arises.

This surrender is the expression of devotional Love and facilitates the de-identification of the "I" with form. Through constant practice, a shift between what one believes to be and the "I" is facilitated. Surrender to Love then takes this a step further in that the "I" itself is surrendered to the Divine; with the "I" falling away, everything else is surrendered. With no "I" left, there is only Love. This surrender to Love transports one from the identification as an individual self with a body and a mind to the realm of non-dual Love—the very essence of Divinity.

Integrity is the cornerstone of all spiritual endeavors and without it the power of Love is not available for spiritual progress. Integrity is ensured by radical honesty, keeping one's agreements, and the understanding that one is always accountable to Love. Another cornerstone of a living spirituality is its expression in form. While spirituality can take infinite forms—prayer, meditation, an evening review—contemplation as well as regular retreats and a spiritual community are time-honored, effective means of transformation. One of the most effective cornerstones of a living spirituality is spiritual guidance or spiritual counseling in which a person is supported step by step into the realization that Love is all that exists.

---

2 Mentalization is experiencing on the mental field.
   This includes thoughts, daydreaming, images, memories.

JAKOB MERCHANT

2
PRINCIPLE

Humility
–The Key to All Spiritual Evolution

INVITATION

I don't know; show me Thy Love

"

I was walking in the University of Salzburg, and a white light begin to shine forth from everything. All the walls, stairs, wood, and people were now suffused by this Light that was only Love. This arose out of the humility to not presume that my experience is reality.

"

[REV. JAKOB MERCHANT]

The key to all spiritual evolution is humility. Humility is a requirement for any spiritual progress, and without it no progress is possible. Nothing supersedes its importance and benefit to the spiritual journey. Its cultivation and development facilitates spiritual growth in every area and aspect of life, including all spiritual practices. With absolute humility, the "I" itself dissolves into Love. It is only vanity that the "I" believes itself to be separate from Love. Humility replaces the "I" and its expression as will, positions taken, perceptions, concepts, opinions, thoughts, and emotions with the reality of Love. Hence, humility is an impersonal divine quality that facilitates the replacing of the illusions of "I" with the reality of Infinite Love. Continuously asking to be led from the illusions of the "I" to the reality of illumined Love transcends perception. One then experiences Love in all that exists as a Light that radiates from it, and more importantly, as a Light that is beyond all form, not different from what one is. All that is required is for the "I" to end its imposition on reality by accepting that it does not know. This radical blank slate is what Love will write on.

Humility is summarized in "I don't know." This continuous attitude of "I don't know" creates the space for the Divine to transfigure, transform, and illuminate. Practicing humility ends any presumptions and the "I" ends superimposing over reality. It is the end of all opinions, beliefs, and positions about anything.

When one lives in a state of humility, any notions of "I know that" as well as any certainty of opinions are terminated. In the radical openness of unknowingness, the illusions of the mind no longer hold. Thoughts have been recognized as fallacious, and it is revealed that the mind is incapable of experiencing the Truth of Love. A prayer such as "I know nothing about this but my illusions; show Thy Truth in their place" will reveal the Truth of Love.

One moves from seemingly knowing to unknowing to reality. Eventually, all of life is transformed into the direct experience of Love because the overlaying of an "I" has ended. Hence, humility is the realization that everything is Divine, and with that, nothing is more or less lovable or better than anything else. All is an equal manifestation of Love. One is here then to witness and be that Love that is the same in all. One merely surrenders to Love in whatever the moment holds, because whatever the moment holds, it holds Love. No positions are possible in the reality of the Light of Love.

From moment to moment, the "I" gives itself to Love out of a sincere acknowledgment of not knowing. Out of an absolute humility arises the willingness to surrender to Love. Humility is, therefore, a critical component of surrender to Love. The "I," and especially the mind, cannot know reality. When the illusion of "I" is replaced by illumination, the Light of Love shines forth from all that exists.

3

PRINCIPLE

Intention
–The Mechanism of Spirituality

I N V I T A T I O N

What is my intention in this moment?

66

*When I practiced spiritual principles such as in A Course in
Miracles, I would remain with a lesson until it manifested in the
world. Every thought was replaced with the lesson until a feeling,
or tone, of that principle replaced the verbalization of the prayer.
It had become pure intention. Then I would continue to hold it
in mind silently until the experience of life was transformed into
whatever the teaching was.*

99

[REV. JAKOB MERCHANT]

JAKOB MERCHANT

To be spiritual is an intention. Intention is part of the mechanism of creation and inherently an impersonal quality of Consciousness. It allows for what is held in the mind persistently to become an experiential reality, a manifestation within the world.

Spirituality then is the practice of consistent intention; this is a focused awareness also known as attention. Everything is transformed into a living spirituality by the intention that is held within and not any outer specific form. It is intention that sanctifies the moment or spiritual practices, and not the practice itself. Every moment is then recontextualized as an opportunity and invitation to hold that spiritual intention. Because where attention goes, energy flows. In other words, spiritual energy is built up via consistent focus. This is often referred to as "one pointedness of mind." It happens naturally when there is a full alignment of all parts of the mind into one laser-like intention that holds no secondary intentions. One knows when the mind is unified and completely aligned as one intention because it will manifest in the world. It is therefore intention that determines destiny.

The critical aspect is to focus on one's intention at any given moment and not on the content of life. That is, we must focus on how every experience, every moment, and every action is held within. "Where is one's focus?" is a question that will lead to where one's intentions are. Once the answer to the question is that one is solely fixated on the spiritual practice, transfiguration will occur. As intention becomes continuous, every moment and aspect of life is transformed. This living spirituality then transforms one's experienced reality into the infinite reality of the Divine. With focus on one's intention instead of form, all exceptions held in the mind dissolve and one lives in the truth that everything is Divine and the "I" is a baseless vanity.

Spirituality as intention takes several forms. Prayer is intention. Prayer and intention may be used interchangeably. The repetitive use of a prayer facilitates its intention to come into manifestation. Utilizing a formal verbal prayer, for example "invoking the Lord," makes a prayer most effective as it not only acknowledges Divinity as the source of all of creation but also describes one's relationship to it. This in turn guarantees the answering of one's prayer because the sole source of all power is being acknowledged and utilized. Another form of intention is to hold it nonverbally; especially as thoughts and the mind are transcended intentions are held silently. This is akin to a sense or a feeling that is continuously held in the silent space. It is as effective to verbalize an intention as it is to hold it nonverbally. Visualization can also be used as an expression of intention. The highest form of intention is summarized as "What is Love's will?" or surrender to Love. Hence, the most effective intention is surrender and in particular surrender to Love. Eventually one's beingness becomes the prayer instead of a specific verbalization. This is particularly true as illumination becomes more and more predominant. Being the radiance of Love then is the prayer in itself and nothing further is needed.

4

PRINCIPLE

Consistency and Unconditional Practice Bring Freedom

INVITATION

I am focused consistently on my spiritual evolution

"

I continued to relentlessly practice the spiritual practice. I was not aware what was going on around me, nor could I recollect anything that was happening. All of my attention and awareness was completely absorbed within the spiritual practice despite the body's seemingly engaged state. What happened in the world had become irrelevant. Awareness had drawn away from form and on to the practice of surrender itself.

"

[REV. JAKOB MERCHANT]

Almost any spiritual practice applied consistently at all times irrespective of circumstance leads to the transcendence of form. No matter what arises in Consciousness, there is always the one and only response—the spiritual practice or intention chosen. Because everything that arises in Consciousness is treated the same way, the content or form has become irrelevant. This automatic response that had been entrained within the mind facilitates a shift of relationship between the sense of "I" and form. This shift is freedom from form, as the "I" has gone beyond it. One is no longer the subject or slave to form but instead the one that lives independently from the world. Consistency and unconditional application are more powerful for one's spiritual transformation than anything else, including the choice of one's spiritual practice or spiritual truth.

It is said that mastery in any area requires about ten thousand hours of practice. Spiritual work then must become a focused, all-in way of living in order for transfiguration to occur. When practicing any spiritual principle, the exceptions to the practice create one's spiritual pathway. One merely needs to examine where exceptions are made to the spiritual aspirations and he or she will know precisely where spiritual progress can be made. The unconditional application can be made systematically by consciously examining where exceptions are being made. This can be through the practice of mindfulness throughout the day, or each evening in a more formal written review that examines the application of one's spiritual life and the exceptions that had been made throughout the day. In this way, the fulcrum of spiritual work is uncovered and the most direct pathway revealed.

Spiritual evolution becomes effortless when one has become whole-hearted, devoted to Love. Having all aspects of one's being completely aligned with the one intention of Love's will brings about spiritual transformation. The key is to not focus on the content of the spiritual work, but instead how one relates to that work. In examining "who" is not aligned with the reality of Infinite Love, it will be discovered that the "I" that is willful has no reality.

JAKOB MERCHANT

5

PRINCIPLE

The Personal Will as the Fulcrum to Enlightenment

INVITATION

Lord, surrender everything as it arises for me

66

Not knowing intellectually what surrender meant, I was praying 'Lord, surrender everything as it arises for me.' I would make sure that every single moment I was holding this intention. Every single thought was replaced with this prayer, and eventually this white Light would begin to shine forth from within.

99

[REV.JAKOB MERCHANT]

The personal will is what determines spiritual evolution via the mechanism of intention. One's will is the only focus one needs to direct one's spiritual aspirations. The personal will or willfulness is the only aspect that stands in the way of any spiritual evolution and a living spirituality. The personal will is a faculty and capacity within Consciousness. Every perception, emotion, belief, thought, concept, or experience is held in place because of the will; every obstacle that one encounters on the entire spiritual evolution is based on the premise that one has a will. With no will, there are no obstacles. Hence, to focus on the will itself is the most direct way to a living spirituality. The personal will is the one and only aspect that keeps the "I" as one's existence in place. It is solely the will that perpetuates the "I." With the dissolving of the will, the "I" also ends. When there is no will, there is only Love.

Surrender is the relinquishment of personal will. With the end of this illusionary will comes the experiential realization that everything happens autonomously without an "I" being involved. This is the case because with continuous surrender, the relationship to form changes. All of form is held in place in Consciousness by the will's manifestation of that particular experience of it. Surrender is to give up one's will and God replaces it with the will of the Divine, which is Love. Surrender is then the act of replacing illusions with reality. It is an act of radical humility that acknowledges that one does not know, and out of a deep and unending devotion that is greater than the individual self, leaves one's will behind. This mechanism where the individual will has ended about everything automatically guarantees the Self to shine forth as the Purusha, or inner Light, because the identification as "I" has been removed, surrendered to God.

There are several forms of willfulness. Willfulness can be experienced as resistance. Experience is only possible if what is experienced is resisted. Once the inherent will with its belief systems are dissolved, Love will shine forth into all experiences, and their form will become irrelevant. The will also can express itself as an attachment such as an attraction or an aversion. The relinquishment of attractions and aversions is the step wise relinquishment of personal will, which immediately brings freedom in that one is no longer subject to the illusionary bondage of specific attractions or aversions. One important spiritual practice then is to continuously examine one's attractions and aversions, and to relinquish them, allowing the glory of Love to take their place.

6

PRINCIPLE

Love is The Ultimate Reality

INVITATION

Love is the ultimate reality

"

In childhood a nightmare would haunt me night after night;
I would be sucked into a black hole and become nothingness.
As a teenager practicing Buddhist meditation, I would enter
consciously over and over an infinite empty space, asking myself
'Is this the ultimate reality?' Only years later, when Dr. David R.
Hawkins looked into my eyes and said that I could stay in the Void
forever[3], the secret allegiance toward the pathway of negation and
its seeming ultimate reality as great emptiness was broken. I was
free to embrace Love.

"

[REV. JAKOB MERCHANT]

---

3 David R.Hawkins, personal communication. 2007

JAKOB MERCHANT

A living, inspired life is one that is filled with Love. Spirituality, Love, and the Divine are interchangeable, inseparable and one and the same. In order to be spiritual, in order to be the Divine, one merely needs to be Love. Love is the fire that fuels all spiritual evolution. No matter what spiritual practice or pathway one follows, all spiritual progress hinges on Love. Focusing, therefore, on that Love has a cataclysmic effect on one's spiritual journey because attention is directed where it needs to be directed. Therefore, Love is not only the ultimate reality and the ultimate spiritual destiny but the only mechanism to realize it.

The spiritual journey is a letting go of beliefs of what Love is into the realization that it is the substrate of all that exists. It then manifests from the completely formless into illumination—the Light of Love—to physical form. As the identification of the "I" shifts and changes, so does the understanding of what Love is. Initially it may be experienced as a local physical phenomenon associated with specific conditions such as other people or activities. Physical Love is predominant when one is identified and attached to physicality; romantic and sexual love, when one is identified as a person. While all Love is Divine Love, at this stage, it is still limited to specific experiences within form. The Pathway of Love is to expand the experience of love from wherever one is to the infinite.

Lovingness is a way on how one relates with form; this means that whatever is experienced one's response to it is lovingness. This then applied consistently dissolves all conditions or positions one holds about form, thereby freeing Consciousness. Love initially is conditional and only allowed to be experienced when the mind's concepts, beliefs, and positions are met. As positions dissolve into Love, Love's experience expands until the position of perception itself dissolves into Divine Light. The ultimate position taken is the position of an "I" separate from Love. With this one dissolving, Love than is the only thing left to exist, not different than what one is.

7
PRINCIPLE

Surrender to Love
—Giving One's Self to Love

INVITATION

I surrender to Love

"

With the intention to give my life entirely and without reservation to the Lord, the Divine, I walked up the stairs and sat down. At that moment, the whole world faded away; all of form faded away, and I was suffused by this golden light that was only Love, the only thing that existed. I gave my life to this; I surrendered to Love.

"

[REV. JAKOB MERCHANT]

JAKOB MERCHANT

The highest form of spirituality is to give one's self as life itself to Love. This devotional offering of one's life to the Divine without any reservations or compartmentalization allows for the "I" to be replaced by Infinite Love. This is a dissolving of the "I" into Infinite Love, which is the essence of Surrender to Love. It is a devotional act where love for Love is greater than for one's self. Out of this unrestricted Love, everything is left behind to be non-dual Love; A Love without the illusion of "I". The world, perception, experiences, the mind, emotions, and most prominently the will itself are all left behind as the "I" dissolves into the Infinite Presence of Love.

As a contemplative practice then, one intends to surrender to Love in every moment and thereby not only continuously dissolves the "I" into Love but also surrenders everything to the Grace of Love. The fulcrum of the process is the will. Surrender to Love is giving up the will in its entirety, but especially the will to be a separate "I." With no will left, there is only Love. Willfulness is replaced with surrender, and the door swings open to the revelations of Divine Love. Surrender to Love is going beyond the individual self as well as its manifestation as the will. It is the will that holds everything in place and with its removal the identification as "I" ceases and is replaced with the ultimate reality.

Beyond the individual self lies the non-dual Love which is Light. This Light of Love, known as illumination, replaces the self. This process of being the Light is a process where the "I" is continuously dissolved into that Love. No matter what content is within Consciousness, one single-heartedly holds the intention of piercing through the illusions of perception and dissolves into that Love that lies beyond it. The Light of Love then replaces the mind's experience of perception. Illumination replaces thinkingness and the sense of an individual's self. This Light then manifests as the world and can be experienced, shining forth from all of this world. Illumination is what is reality, and that illumined Love is eternal, never changing, and non-dual.

In each moment, then, the intention is to realize the ultimate reality that Love is all, Love is all that exists by Surrendering to that Love. One knows when it is complete because nothing is left but Love itself.

While surrender is an ending of the individual will, Surrender to Love is a dissolving of the "I" into Infinite Love. They are interrelated processes. As the "I" dissolves, the will dissolves with it, and with no will, no illusions of an "I" ever existed. The mechanism, however, is different in that surrender removes the illusion of the "I" by relinquishing the will and thereby allowing for the reality of Divine autonomous manifestation. Surrender to Love is a Love that is stronger than the "I" and with that dissolves the "I" from its imaginary existence, creating the space for reality to shine forth on its own.

JAKOB MERCHANT

8

PRINCIPLE

The "I" and Its Identifications

INVITATION

Lord, dissolve the sense of I

66

When returning from the retreat, thoughts would come back and arise, however a shift in relationship to thoughts and thinkingness had happened. They were no longer my thoughts.

99

[REV. JAKOB MERCHANT]

Everything within this world—every thought, every feeling, every emotion, every action and interaction between people—is an autonomous manifestation of Love. There is no "I," or self, and hence, the "I" doesn't cause anything in the world. All of form is a continuous creation of Love where everything happens by itself based on its inherent nature.

The "I" is an illusion and identification. It is identified initially with form such as being a person, being thoughts, emotions, or the doer of deeds. This is an experiential distortion of reality where the Divine manifests itself as all of form, whereas the "I" merely claims being these things until reality has replaced that claim.

One of the most critical aspects of one's spiritual evolution is the shift in identification of the "I." This shift of who one believes, feels, and experiences to be is the essence of the pathway through Consciousness into the awareness that Love is the substrate and manifestation of all that exists.

One of the first shifts of the identification of the "I" is the de-identification to form. The relationship to form is the critical aspect of spiritual focus and one's spiritual evolution. It is not the form or content itself that needs to be addressed but the relationship one has with it.

Ultimately, as the "I" no longer is identified with form, form no longer has an effect on what one used to be identified with. All of form comes and goes according to its nature, Love's creation, and one is free from it as one no longer is subject to it. The identification of the "I" has shifted into subtler states of awareness such as witnessing or even Consciousness and awareness itself. As with the other layers of identification, the "I" is merely a superposition of witnessing or Consciousness. These are also autonomous processes of a manifestation from the source of all that exists.

The "I" continues to be removed from wherever it is identified with until only the "I" as existence itself remains. Just as before, whenever the "I" was removed from its identifications, a seemingly dying of the old occurred. This is now at the center and forefront. With the "I" allowing itself to completely die, it is replaced by Infinite Love, the source out of which everything arises.

This dying is softened by the immensity of that Love. The Love is so strong that the "I" melts and dissolves into it.

All aspects of life, then, are autonomous processes from the most concrete content to greater and greater context. The very source of all of life is revealed to be unmanifested Love, which radiates forth within all that exists. And when one dissolves the sense of "I," one witnesses this Glory of Love unfolding.

9

PRINCIPLE

Integrity
—One is Always Accountable to Love

INVITATION

One is always accountable to Love

❝

How could 'I' be responsible if that 'I' had no power over the body's actions? If only form is subject to consequences, what about Consciousness? Eventually I realized that just because one is not identified with the body, one still is responsible for it, akin to a pet that one has adopted.

❞

[REV. JAKOB MERCHANT]

JAKOB MERCHANT

Integrity is the cornerstone of the spiritual journey. Without it no spiritual life is possible. It consists of several components, all of which not only facilitate spiritual progress but more importantly are safeguards to it. Without integrity there is no space in which the Love of the Divine can permanently be experienced. Integrity can be defined as being accountable to Love.

Integrity consists of several aspects, or components, all of which are critical to spirituality and life in general. First and foremost, integrity is an internal consistency where one has determined a moral way of living, and with radical honesty examines every action and behavior, takes complete responsibility for those actions and behaviors, and realigns toward these principles.

Integrity therefore includes adhering to an ethical or moral code. Morality is summarized in what is most loving and thereby serving the highest good of all that exists. The answer to the question of "What is the most Loving?" provides a guideline that can be applied in any situation or circumstance. In-depth moral codes are provided by all of the world religions, and any one of them is sufficient to safeguard a living spirituality.

On the spiritual journey it is critical to take responsibility for everything that happens within one's experience of life without exception. What is held in mind, consciously or subconsciously, tends to manifest as one's experience and therefore one always knows what is held within the mind by examining one's life. Whatever is currently present in one's life is a perfect mirror for what is held within, which includes what one perceives as obstacles, struggles, or vicissitudes. And it can only be corrected within, by the Divine Presence. Nothing "out there" has any power, as all power comes from Divinity itself and is then channeled through the filters of the mind into one's experiential reality.

Another aspect of integrity is to keep the agreements that one has made both with oneself and others. Breaking agreements, regardless of with whom they were made, always decreases spiritual power and the ability to use the Divine Presence. While it is often more obvious that one has broken agreements to others, agreements, commitments or decisions made to one's self are even more important. Without them, one cannot live constantly in the presence of Divinity within.

Honesty itself is an expression of Love. Honesty requires the courage to stand in the Truth of Love instead of illusions. Honesty is both a pathway to the Divine and a requirement for any spiritual evolution. This is expressed preeminently in self-honesty. Self-honesty reveals the illusions that can be dissolved into the Light of Love. The highest form of honesty is that the "I" is nothing but an illusion and Love is all that exists. Another form of honesty is authenticity in which one's internal experience and outer expression are one and the same. Here integrity takes the form of the courage to tell the truth about one's self. This owning of the truth allows for the Truth to reveal itself. Integrity is an automatic consequence of telling the truth about one's self. One's integrity can therefore be regained when one owns the truth about oneself. Hence, this principle can be summarized as "to Thy own Self be true."

Integrity is the shift of focus from being primarily self-focused and self-centered to being Love centered; that is, focused on the highest good and welfare of all that exists. When the experiential reality and needs, wishes, and desires of others are honored, they no longer are merely a means to an end. Love has expanded to the realization that one is here to give one's self to that Love as expressed as others.

10

PRINCIPLE

Spiritual Practices and Applications

INVITATION

I am practicing spiritual principles at all times

"

One reoccurring experience throughout childhood was the Light of Love or illumination. In my first spiritual counseling session with Rev. Diane Berke, she pointed out to me that there still was a subtle sense of separation between me and that Light. The focus of the spiritual practice needed to be on dissolving the "I" who was experiencing illumination, as well as the identification of "I" as Consciousness. This insight propelled my spiritual evolution and could only arise from a spiritual guide that could lead me outside my own belief systems. This leading outside one's paradigm of reality is the hallmark of spiritual counseling.

"

[REV. JAKOB MERCHANT]

Meditation and Contemplation

The purpose of meditation is to transcend the identification with "I." Along the spiritual journey there are infinite forms of meditation. Those that serve the "I" to be dissolved into Infinite Love are the most effective and most important. Other forms of meditation may serve a specific purpose supporting a living spirituality. Meditation is persistent intention. While its form may differ, the intention determines its effectiveness. Eventually meditation becomes contemplation, when one meditates at all times and circumstances even with one's eyes open and the body interacting with the world.

Tracking and Evening Review

A way to guarantee and safeguard one's spirituality is to track the qualities or aspects that are important to one's spiritual life and to review them daily. Observation and mindfulness, as well as tracking one's spiritual ideals, have been proven to guarantee one's spiritual progress. It is a continuous realigning of one's life to the compass of one's spiritual vision. Qualities to track can be any that one chooses. For a living spirituality, aspects such as attractions, aversions, reading of sacred texts, surrender, meditation and contemplation, as well as exceptions to lovingness, honesty, and integrity can be measured on a daily basis. It is then the power of Consciousness itself that will change what one is observing consistently. An evening review also allows one to make peace with the past; doing so prevents one from carrying anything into the next moment or day. This clearing of what happened on a daily basis eventually creates deep freedom, love, and peace as one is no longer connected to what happens.

Spiritual Community

Spiritual community is of critical importance on one's spiritual journey. One not only becomes the average of the people one is associated with, but more importantly these people are the source of inspiration and a vessel of Love's guidance in one's life. The people in one's life can strongly influence one's spiritual destiny. It is critical to assess the people in one's life in the context of their impact on one's spiritual life. Ideally, they are not only supporting the application of all spiritual principles described in this book but they also raise the spiritual standards around oneself. People are an opportunity to expand one's love unconditionally, and eventually they are an avenue on how to surrender to Love.

Spiritual Guidance

One of the most valuable supports toward a living spirituality is spiritual guidance, direction, or counseling. This allows not only for help, support, and accountability while one embarks on a spiritual journey but also most often expands one's perception to a greater understanding that would have not been possible otherwise. All great spiritual teachings recommend the support of a person on the spiritual journey whether it be a priest, spiritual teacher, guide, or spiritual friend who supports the application of spirituality into one's life. The spiritual guide becomes also the physical manifestation of the Grace of Love; one calls forth this transmission of Love by intention and Divine radiance will transform, transfigure and illuminate a person into Love.

A Daily Routine

Persistence, or a continuous ongoing spiritual life and practice, is of more value than sporadic practices. A daily spiritual routine and habit can support one's overall spiritual evolution facilitating a living spirituality. It is best developed with an experienced guide such as a spiritual counselor. An accountability partner from one's spiritual community further ensures that one's spiritual intentions become an experiential reality.

Retreats—A Time for Transformation and Preparation

On the spiritual journey, rarely anything compares to the spiritual value of retreats. Setting aside time and context for dedicated spiritual work is more important than anything else. Retreats allow for the outer world and outer context to be set aside so that one can completely focus within, allowing for deeper aspects to surface. It is at this time that deep transformation and change occurs. While some aspects of spirituality can be learned only in the world, others can be learned only when one is completely removed from it. This may include honing specific aspects of spirituality that then can be translated into daily life.

Other retreats focus on perfecting specific spiritual topics such as unconditional love or surrender to Love. It is always time to deepen the connection and direct experience with the Divine more than ever before. At retreats, outer silence can become inner silence, and experiencing the mind or limiting identifications can be transcended. Regular retreats throughout the year integrate both worlds into a truly living spirituality. Anybody who is serious about their spiritual evolution will integrate retreats into their overall life. Eventually sporadic retreats become ingrained, and one's whole life is recontextualized as one retreat. Everything has been set aside in order to realize the Truth of Love. The retreat is no longer external but instead internal.

Appendix & Further

Resources

How to Stay Connected

How to stay connected with Rev. Jakob Merchant

We hope that this book stands in completeness by itself. However, an expansion on the core principles outlined in this book may be helpful to the reader. Even more so, a spiritual community and a spiritual guide can be of invaluable benefit. In this section are further resources provided for one's spiritual journey. On the following pages, one can find a description and contact information for these services. If you have questions of any kind, please do not hesitate to contact us.

Find out how to connect to all of Rev. Jakob's work at

www.jakobmerchant.com

Surrender to Love -the Heart of Non-Duality

Surrender to Love is the heart and essence of Reverend Jakob Merchant's lifelong journey and available as an in-depth online course, group workshop, and group and individual retreats at Communion with Love and the Sedona Surrender Retreat House. It is also expanded upon in his forthcoming book, **Surrender to Love—the Heart of Non-Duality.**

Would you like to experience more Love?

Have you longed for Love?

Have you realized that Love is the highest value in your life?

Then you are ready to Surrender to Love.

Surrender to Love is for everyone who would like to seek the experience of Love everywhere. It is written for the spiritual person who seeks the pathway of non-dual Love in order to dissolve the self with its will and replace it with the Infinite Presence of Love. Surrender to Love is intended for those who seek to become the essence of Divinity, the very heart of the Lord of Love.

Surrender to Love is for those who are seeking a direct experience with Love. It is not an intellectual teaching but merely an exchange of one's self for Love. It is a spiritual practice where the self is replaced with Divine Love. Hence it is most suitable for those who would like to choose Love above one's self.

What if there is a Love that is so great that nothing else matters? A Love that is so complete that each moment in and of itself is complete. A Love that is so great that one merely dissolve into it and "dies into Love." A Love that is beyond all form, beyond everything that exists. Surrender to Love is the path to experience that Love in every moment, to experience it as the only thing that exists, and finally, as what one is. When Love becomes one's only goal, one is willing to give one's self to Love and begin the journey into non-dual Love, which is the journey of Surrender to Love.

What Impact has Surrender to Love had?

"

Jakob, your lessons have led me to such peace. It may have been a particular way you phrased something, or how you shared your Loving intentions, or how you pointed us and guided us—all of which wove an embrace that allowed for a more peaceful and integrated courage to come forward. It was a bringing out of what has always been—before our very existence, before time—pulling me forward. When I think of what you have given us in this very short time, I thank you and I am most grateful.

"

[DONNA HOLLMAN OF NELSON, CANADA]

You can find more information here:

communionwithlove.com/product/surrendertolove

communionwithlove.com/surrender-to-love

JAKOB MERCHANT

Unconditional Love–A Love that does not Want to Change Anything will Change Everything

Unconditional Love is a Love that just is. It has no requirements, hence one is free to Love. It is Love that can be experienced independently of circumstances. It is a Love that has moved from an emotion to a state of being. A Love that has become the backdrop of one's existence. Our work on unconditional Love answers the following prayer:

I want to know what Love is, I want Love to show me.

I want to feel what Love is, come and show me.

This unconditional Love not only allows for a permanent experience of Love but also facilitates healing. In the context of unconditional Love, the safety is created to allow for anything to be healed in the sunlight of Love. Therefore one can come to our unconditional Love programs with issues or problems and apply that Love toward them, because feeling loved facilitates transformation.

What if there is a space and a place to experience Love no matter what may happen in one's life? What if there was a place where Divine Love envelops you and guides you into an experience of that Love so that you leave changed and transformed by the transformational power of Love itself? Leaving behind the attachments and suffering that stem from a lack of Love in one's life, one learns to allow oneself to be fully and totally loved so one eventually becomes that very Love.

Unconditional Love is a context and backdrop of everything that Rev. Jakob does and is a part of all workshops, retreats, and courses. The programs directly dedicated to it, however, focus on deepening one's Love in one's life permanently and utilizing that Love for healing, change, and spiritual evolution.

Would you like to deepen the experience of Love in your life?

Would you like to feel loved and use that Love for healing

and transformation?

Would you like to end the suffering that stems from

a lack of Love in your life?

Then you are ready to immerse yourself in

unconditional Love!

What Impact has the Unconditional Love Course had?

”

If you have the great good fortune to have been led here to this review, I wholeheartedly urge you to just go for it now! At the very least, order and practice the Introduction Session. Don't even think about it anymore. The experience is beyond words. Suffice it to say that the description of the Healing Intensive above is what occurs within. Of course, you must do what is asked of you. This course is one of the most intense (it's called an "Intensive" for a reason) inner life-changing experiences I have ever been through. I am so very grateful that I let go of my financial fear and my concern about it taking up too much of my time. The reason? Because I am now a new person, a person I am thankful for: more peaceful, patient, kind, forgiving, compassionate, and unconditionally loving than I was two months before I started this course. My inner, lasting, daily subjective experience confirms this to be true. It's the beginning of a more conscious, continuous journey of letting go. It has profoundly changed my daily practice, no, my very being. These inner changes would most likely have occurred eventually; however, I am convinced that the profound changes within would have taken many, many years or even lifetimes. In short, I love this course and I Love You

Much Love and many blessings on your journey.

“

[CHRIS O HARE OF ASHEVILLE, NORTH CAROLINA]

Online Courses - Integrating Spirituality into One's Life

Online courses allow one to integrate spiritual principles into daily life as one experiences them in the environment in which one normally lives. Rev. Jakob Merchant offers many different online courses on spiritual and healing topics ranging from ten-day courses to year-long intensives. Some of them, such as the ones on the sacred texts, are free of charge.

Find a listing of current online courses here:

communionwithlove.com/product-category/courses

10 Days to a Living Spirituality online course

10 Days to a Living Spirituality is the companion online course that puts the ten principles of this book into practice and deepens them. Just as this book reveals the essence of a living spirituality, the course puts them all into practice and makes them alive. The course includes a daily lesson, guided meditation, and videos for each lesson.

Sign up for the course here:

communionwithlove.com/product/
10-days-to-a-living-spirituality

Spiritual Counseling–The Direct Path to One's Own Journey of a Living Spirituality

In spiritual counseling, a companionship is formed, where in the safe environment of unconditional Love, spirituality is developed and deepened, so that one can experience peace of mind, a sense of belonging, and a feeling of being loved.

Through spiritual counseling, one learns to look at a given situation and answer to the question:

"Where is Love in this?"

Spiritual counseling may be for you if you would like to ...

... find a safety and security in God that allows you to bring spirituality into your daily life. After you have made peace with yourself and the world, and because you are Love, you will feel loved. You are committed to finding a spiritual solution to life's problems, and with the help of your spiritual counselor, you continue to deepen that spirituality. You experience the perfection, sacredness, and Divinity of all things. You are the Light.

Rev. Jakob on spiritual counseling:

Among all spiritual tools, spiritual counseling has been the most valuable aspect of my own spiritual journey. To have someone to journey with in deep Love for each other that can support and, at times, guide is of more value than any spiritual text or teaching. The individual advice, teaching, and most importantly Love received from my own spiritual counselor and teachers has propelled my spiritual evolution in ways otherwise unimaginable. Ultimately Love itself is the teacher, and one can connect to this teaching quality of Love in any moment. At the same time, Love's manifestation as a spiritual counselor is one of the greatest blessings of Love one can have in a lifetime.

Experience with Spiritual Counseling

"

I had been praying to meet a spiritual guide that I could travel with in this lifetime. Somehow I knew that I needed a spiritual teacher that I could receive guidance from directly, rather than through books, lectures, or courses. Then one day I found myself at a meditation at the home of Jakob Merchant. From the moment I saw him, I knew from the depths of my being that he was the one I had been praying for. I have often found that to simply sit in his presence and receive the silent transmission of Love is enough for the answers and assistance to come into my awareness. I am eternally grateful for the blessing that is his friendship, his guidance, his Love. He is an emanation of Love itself.

"

[JENINE GOBBI OF SEDONA, ARIZONA]

JAKOB MERCHANT

Surrender Retreats –Transformation Through Experience

Mission statement

Surrender retreats create moments in one's life that become so impactful that all of life is permanently changed. We provide these transformational experiences that permanently alter one's life via individual, group, and self-guided time away from the world. Some of these experiences are even available from the comfort of one's home. Retreats are filled with the most effective forms of transforming moments that allow a person to move from where they are into where they would like to be. Retreats include therapy, silence, relaxation and rejuvenation, in-depth spiritual work and practices as well as one-on-one guidance for a permanent change that is then translated into one's daily life with ongoing support.

"

When we were about done, I stared into your eyes and felt a peace I have never come close to feeling. You were bringing me closer to God. The trust I felt. I want to come back for hands-on sessions four times a year.

"

[CHRISTY TAYLOR OF AUSTIN, TEXAS]

Rev. Jakob Merchant on Surrender Retreats

Many spiritual breakthroughs arise out of in-depth spiritual retreats. These retreats last from days to more than a year. Deep, intensely dedicated spiritual work facilitates breakthroughs in one's spiritual evolution. These then can be translated into one's daily life via the support of online courses, spiritual counseling, and a connection to other people who share the same devotion—Love's company.

Out of the transformations that retreats provided for me, it arose to provide the same opportunity for others. Having experienced retreats in all of the religious and spiritual traditions, I have incorporated in my own retreats the most effective means from religion and spirituality, as well as psychotherapy and health and healing.

Surrender retreats are typically one- to three-day retreats both for individuals and groups. They focus on what is most pertinent and alive at any given time for a person, in particular spiritual transformation or relieving suffering. Different types of retreats are available.

JAKOB MERCHANT

Types of Retreats

One unique aspect of Surrender retreats is that many are available in individual, group, or self-guided form; some retreats are even available online and can be practiced from the comfort of one's home.

Self-guided Retreats

Self-guided retreats are fully structured retreats that can be done individually without another person. Every piece of the retreat is in writing and also includes recorded audio and video so that a person can follow along without having Rev. Jakob present. In addition to that, several options and choices are given to individualize the retreat. Some pieces of the retreat can be exchanged for working with a spiritual counselor or Rev. Jakob, if he's available.

Group Retreats

Group retreats are intimate gatherings, typically three to five people focusing on one specific topic as a group. The power of the group as well as the group dynamic is used to bring about transformation and the specific experience the group is focused on.

Individual Retreats

Individual retreats are tailored to the needs of the person and directly address the person's path forward in any area of life. These retreats may focus on whatever the person has come for, individualizing a specific topic and applying it into the unique context of the person.

Online Retreats

All three types of retreats—self-guided, group, and individual—are available online. The requirement is to set up an undisturbed context at home (or hotel, as some have done in the past) and have a fully functional internet connection available. The structure of these retreats is identical to in-person retreats. The only difference is that they are experienced from the comfort of one's home. This not only saves traveling costs but also brings the retreat experience where it eventually needs to be—in the context where one lives.

Surrender to Love

Surrender to Love retreats are focused intensives lasting from one to three days in which one learns, practices, and experiences the transformational power of surrendering to Love. Retreats include meditation, contemplation, numerous spiritual practices, reflections and reviews designed to not only transform one's life but also to train one in the art of Surrender to Love. These retreats are customized both to the person or group and an application of Surrender to Love—the heart of non-duality as well as the corresponding online course. Its goal is to help the participant find and experience Love in every moment, no matter what the circumstances or perception. For those who value Love above all else, this retreat is invaluable. At its end stands the realization that Love is all, Love is all that exists.

Unconditional Love

Sometimes in the day-to-day living of one's life, one forgets to reconnect to the Source of Love itself, which is Divinity. The Unconditional Love retreat offers this reconnection with absolute Love so that one can be Love absolutely without reservation, hesitation, or condition. One must allow Love to flow into one's life to become Love. If you are called to "be Love" at all times, no matter what life holds, and to reconnect to that Love as the very source of transformation, please join us for our retreat on Unconditional Love.

Living Spirituality

A living spirituality is a life that is "in Spirit," or inspired; one's spirituality is alive in every moment, not only in sporadic occurrences. The focus of this retreat is how to ensure one's spirituality every day and every moment. Here one brings one's life and spirituality together and integrates them. One also answers the fundamental question, Where is God in this? Applying the most advanced techniques and spiritual practices to one's life and struggles transforms them into the realization that they are the gift of Love. In that space, change then becomes effortless. These retreats also focus on the learning and training necessary for living spirituality, virtually creating a bulwark that is not swayed by the tides of life.

Be the Light

Illumination, being the Light of Love, does not have to be a rare occurrence. This retreat is focused on transcending perception. Once the individual self is dissolved into Love, the divine radiance shines forth on its own. This retreat focuses particularly on transcending the mind's illusions of sensory perceptions to experience the Love that lies underneath. With the ability to open up to this radiance, one eventually discovers that Love is what one is, not a person, or "self." This is then applied to anything in one's life that one did not experience as Love previously so that each moment and memory is illumined. One then leaves being the Light.

Healing Retreats

Healing retreats are designed to transform and heal a person's physical, mental, emotional, and even spiritual struggles, and they incorporate the most effective forms of therapy available. These retreats are designed to permanently reset one's life. While including in-depth inner work, they also typically include training that involves lifestyle changes appropriate to one's life. Most of these retreats are uniquely tailored to the client. They may, for instance, focus on a specific topic such as "Forgiveness, the restoration of the reality of Love" or "Healing the physical."

Sedona Surrender Retreat House

The Sedona Surrender Retreat House is a home dedicated to Love, Surrender, and illumination. It offers a home-like, peaceful, and nurturing environment where guests are welcomed for rest and renewal. It is the host of Communion with Love, the Health and Healing Clinic, and Surrender Retreats in Sedona.

The property is situated on one and a half acres of land with scenic views of the beautiful rock formation known as Cathedral Rock. The property has walking paths to Oak Creek, only five minutes walking distance away.

Located amidst grand Sedona rocks and the sweet sounds of the surrounding state forest, you can immerse yourself in a sanctuary of love and healing.

Stay in touch with us:

www.sedonasurrenderretreats.com

www.facebook.com/Surrenderretreat

Contact us for accommodations or to book a room via our website:

www.surrenderretreats.com

Some Experiences at the Sedona Surrender Retreat House

"This is my fourth stay with Jakob and Fabiola. It was incredible as usual. They have now become family and this is the only place I will stay in Sedona"
[DANIELLE LIPOFF OF AGAWAM, MASSACHUSETTS]

"Truly one of the most amazing places we have yet to stay using Airbnb. We returned again this year and hope to do so again next year."
[MICHELE OF MILWAUKEE, WISCONSIN]

"VERY quiet space and had a "sacred" feel to it."
[LAYTON OF HOUSTON, TEXAS]

"This was the best B and B experience we have had, and we have had a lot."
[ROGER OF BEND, OREGON]

"Fabiola & Jakob's place is everything you could ask for and more!"
[BRIANA OF WANTAGH, NEW YORK]

"I cannot recommend staying with Fabiola and Jakob enough! They are beyond warm and welcoming. The space is so tranquil and has access to awesome trails. Yoga with Jakob was amazing and ended up being the perfect spot to watch the sunset. I will absolutely stay there again!"
[GRACE OF CHICAGO, ILLINOIS]

"This place will exceed your expectations!"
[LAYTON OF HOUSTON, TEXAS]

"Fabulous. Perfect place to stay in Sedona. Highly recommend. We loves every moment in this beautiful space!"
[JILL OF NEW YORK, NEW YORK]

"Fabiola and Jakob's home is a tranquil retreat center with every amenities you could need. They are kind and resourceful in guiding my stay at Sedona. I wish I had more time to stay in the property. I love this part of town. Looking forward to return"
[GLENDY OF NEW YORK, NEW YORK]

"A spiritual dream come true. Love the property inside and out."
[DONNA VALENTINE OF KIHEI, HAWAII]

"It's the perfect place to find your balance."
[JOVAN OF CHICAGO, ILLINOI]

"Second time staying with Jakob and Fabiola. We love their peaceful home so much we can't wait to come back."
[ERIKA, UNITED STATES]

"Perfect if you want peace and quiet."
[KELIE OF FAIRFIELD, OHIO]

"If you are looking for your own beautiful spiritual retreat space with loads of silence in a divine nature location... this is It! Stunning views of Cathedral Rock."
[PIXY OF FLAGLER BEACH, FLORIDA]

"What a wonderful and peaceful place!"
[LEX OF MIAMI, FLORIDA]

"Fabiola and Jakob have cultivated a home that is filled with love and positive energy, and guests will notice it as soon as they walk into the tranquil garden area."
[TERRI OF LONG BEACH, CALIFORNIA]

"This is my second trip staying with Fabiola and Jakob and I can't wait to return."
[ELIANA OF CHAMPAIGN, ILLINOIS]

"Feels like coming home! I can just recommend anyone to stay with Fabiola and Jakob. After two days, I left Sedona with new energy and full of inspiration"
[CLARA ANTONIA OF MUNICH, GERMANY]

"The yoga retreat was everything I had hoped for and more. A truly peaceful loving and nurturing space, one I was sad to leave."
[KIM OF CAPE TOWN, SOUTH AFRICA]

JAKOB MERCHANT

"If I could rate this place an 11 out of 5 stars I would."
[CAROLINA OF MEDELLIN, COLOMBIA]

"Perfect place if you desire to get quiet and go deep."
[BECKY OF BALDWIN, MARYLAND]

"We love staying here and feels like family."
[MARCI OF SCOTTSDALE, ARIZONA]

"This is the most peaceful space I have ever been."
[TANYA OF SOUTH HAVEN, MICHIGAN]

"We participated to one of Jakob's beautifully led community worship services & found it to be very calming & mindful. It was an hour of meditation & peace- with beautiful music.... a good stay for the soul"
[TANYA OF BATON ROUGE, LOS ANGELES]

"We loved Fabiola and Jakob place. Beautiful, clean, positive energy. It was such a great experience. We are definitely looking forward to be back."
[NADIA OF KILLEEN, TEXAS]

"I had an absolute beautiful time here. The room was so serene, comfortable and lovely. Fabiola and Jakob are wonderful hosts and such amazing energies. I felt like I was in my own world. I will definitely come here again soon."
[VANESSA OF JERSEY CITY, NEW JERSEY]

"If you want an accommodation that is consistent with a relaxing and even spiritual experience in Sedona, then Fabiola and Jakob's residence is the place for you. The rooms and bathrooms are clean, private, peaceful and transcendent."
[JAMES OF NAPA, CALIFORNIA]

"Fabiola and Jakob have intentionally created a place for their guest's tranquility and peace. Would stay again in a heartbeat."
[CARA OF CALIFORNIA, UNITED STATES]

"Not only are they one of the kindest people you will meet but everything about their property emanates peace, love, and so much intention."
[CHINA OF MIAMI BEACH, FLORIDA]

"Their backyard alone is a dream and PERFECT for walking meditation."
[AMY OF OMAHA, NEBRASKA]

"This is a beautiful, loving, peaceful space. The hosts are wonderful and kind."
[MILES OF TUCSON, ARIZONA]

JAKOB MERCHANT

Communion with Love - Teaching Others How to Love by Loving Them

Mission statement

Communion with Love seeks to support in the realization of the Presence of Divinity within. Some pathways have called this state "Unio Mystica," "Buddha Nature," "Unmanifest," and "Godhead." We like to call it "Love." In this way, it aims to make spiritual Truth experiential instead of conceptual. Love is the essence of Divinity and therefore the essence of all genuine spiritual pathways, which we seek to support solely for Thy Glory and the greater good of all.

The invitation is to realize one's true Self as Infinite Love

Who We Are

Communion with Love is a 501c3 nonprofit organization dedicated to the deepening of Love in our everyday life. We believe that Love is the fundamental truth of all genuine spiritual pathways and thus our work is not of any particular religious denomination and incorporates many of the great pathways.

Being God's Love to the world

What We Do

We offer a variety of day-long workshops, evening events, and online courses that explore various spiritual topics and pathways, aiming to make one's spiritual truth experiential. We have come to experience that Love is sufficient unto itself and that the increase in lovingness is worth all the effort one can bring to it. Communion with Love offers many workshops, retreats, and daily meditations as well as devotional services free of charge on a donation basis. Most offerings are also available long-distance via live stream.

You can find our current schedule here:

communionwithlove.com/events

Loving you until you become that Love

Our spiritual director and historical context

Communion with Love has formed to bring transformation and direct experience of spiritual truth, especially Love to the world. Historically it emerged out of Reverend Jakob Merchant's call to ministry. After his ordination by One Spirit Interfaith Seminary, he received confirmation and blessings to form this spiritual organization as a vehicle of spiritual transformation.

This inspiration and transformation stems from Love. The most profound experience of Love has come from Dr. David R. Hawkins. We are eternally grateful for that Love that taught us what true Love is. All of our ministry stems from that Absolute Love.

Rev. Jakob on Communion with Love

Many times, when I went to communion, I experienced an infinite white Light. This realization of non-dual Love is what Communion with Love is dedicated to, to be the Light. Years of deep inner spiritual work led to the point where my environment urged me to enter seminary. Initially I was hesitant and not interested. Only after my spiritual teacher affirmed that this was in the best and highest good for all beings did I follow through by entering seminary. I never was interested in teaching spiritual teachings; however, I found great value in helping people make spiritual truth experiential in one's life, especially the direct experience of Love.

Through seminary, I discovered the deep unconditional Love that lies beyond the surface of day-to-day life in all religions and spiritual traditions. A true spirituality is there for everyone, not only a specific denomination or creed. This teaching that "Paths are many but truth is one"[4] is what became the essence of Communion with Love. Communion with Love is a community dedicated to Love irrespectively of any creed, religion, or belief system. All are held as equals in the Light of Love.

Our Dedication and Invocation

My life belongs to Divinity
May the Lord of Love do with it as He pleases
Infinite Love is the creed I hold
Veritas the path I serve
Beauty, Love, and Divinity all that I see
All Glory be to Thee
You may have all of me

Stay in touch with us:

www.communionwithlove.com
www.facebook.com/CommunionWithLove

Join Communion with Love's newsletter:
www.communionwithlove.com/newsletter
Additional social media including YouTube videos can be accessed here:
www.communionwithlove.com/socialmedia

---

4 This quote is commonly attributed to Mahatma Gandhi and Swami Satchidananda

Health and Healing Clinic - Holistic Healing Supporting One's Spiritual Evolution

Mission Statement

The Health and Healing Clinic seeks to relieve suffering in all its forms. It provides holistic healthcare that addresses the physical, mental, emotional, and spiritual needs of our clients. Our dedication is to excellence in everything we do and in utilizing the most effective means of healing.

The clinic has been founded on the premise of Consciousness-based healthcare. This means that all healing comes from within, and a therapist or practitioner simply facilitates what already lies in wait inside. The relief of suffering has been at the core of the clinic. Over the years, the clinic has added the most effective means for therapy to help clients in all areas of life.

Holistic Health and Spirituality

The body is the temple of Love in which the Truth of Love is being remembered. Because the body, and especially the brain, is the processing station of Consciousness, a healthy body can be utilized for a living spirituality. The Health and Healing Clinic is therefore committed to support a body's innate healing ability so that one's focus can remain on one's spiritual evolution.

Rev. Jakob Experiences Around Health and Healing:

The Health and Healing Clinic arose out of the commitment and compassion to relieve suffering of mankind. It is a spiritual mistake to deny the illusions of suffering. It is the clinic's dedication to acknowledge their seeming experiential reality, while directing to the Divine reality beyond.

JAKOB MERCHANT

When practicing a meditation practice to be Love's quality of healing to the world spontaneous healing of the body occurred. A decade old respiratory illness subsided within days of practice. The spiritual dictum to be to others what one wants for oneself, also applies to health and healing. This pathway of the servant of Love recontextualizes the illness and its symptoms, as what one is invited to be to the world. At the heart of the Health and Healing Clinic therefore, stands the realization, that illness is an opportunity to be the source of healing to others.

Operating Principles of The Health and Healing Clinic

- » Unconditional Love facilitates healing.

- » Holistic healing addresses each issue on the physical, mental, energetic, emotional, and spiritual levels.

- » The body is a reflection of the mind; as the mind changes, so does the body.

- » The person who has an illness needs to change in order for it to disappear.

- » Illness always includes suppressed emotions, especially guilt and erroneous belief systems.

- » Environmental changes support health and healing.

- » Consciousness itself knows what is needed for healing; intuition and kinesiology is a means to access this innate wisdom.

- » Surrendering one's will to Divinity activates self-healing.

- » Prayer facilitates healing. We love and pray for our clients.

Experience with The Health and Healing Clinic

"

I have thoroughly enjoyed my sessions with Jakob and have experienced healing of very difficult emotions and memories through my work with him. I highly recommend him for his deep listening and compassionate approach to healing.

"

[DARREN OF PHOENIX, ARIZONA]

Connect with the Health and Healing Clinic:

www.healthandhealingclinic.net

Therapies and System Used at the Health and Healing Clinic

Parama BodyTalk–Consciousness-based healthcare

Parama BodyTalk is one the most comprehensive and effective healing systems in the world today. It is a truly individualized and holistic therapy including treatment on the physical, mental, emotional, energetic, spiritual, and environmental levels. While it can be simplistically summarized as "energy medicine", it is truly Consciousness-based healthcare where a shift in the mind leads to shifts in the body.

An outstanding aspect of BodyTalk is that it is priority based. This means that what a person truly needs at any given point is revealed. Based on intuition, muscle testing, or "kinesiology," it asks what a person needs from innate wisdom, thereby ensuring truly individualized healthcare.

"

You'd be someone I comfortably refer to, and you can quote me on that

"

[JOHN VELTHEIM FOUNDER OF BODYTALK]

BodyTalk includes Western and Eastern forms of medicine as well as aspects of classical psychotherapy, energy medicine, and spirituality. Rev. Jakob has trained the full scope of BodyTalk including extensive training with the founder of BodyTalk John Veltheim; he is an advanced certified practitioner, as well as Parama BodyTalk practitioner.

Ericksonian Therapy and Hypnotherapy

Milton H. Erickson was the most successful psychotherapist of all times. In Ericksonian therapy, an experience for the client is created that changes the client at his core—that is, his state of Consciousness, beliefs, behaviors, and self-image. This form of psychotherapy uses what the client already brings; the therapist creates a solution out of the seeming problem which is the prescribed treatment. It is highly individualized and can be said to invent a new therapy for each client. Hypnotherapy facilitates a state of heightened awareness that maximizes growth and learning. It is one of the primary ways of facilitating change in Ericksonian therapy. Rev. Jakob has extensively trained in the approach of the Erickson Institute in addition to engaging in years of monthly one-on-one training with Jeffrey K. Zeig, the founder and director of the Institute.

Visualization and Imagery

Visualization is a way to express intention prior to thought while addressing the mental plane. It directly connects to the deeper layers of Consciousness, such as the subconscious. Advanced forms of imagery not only become a way to express intention but also a two-way form of communication with these deeper layers of Consciousness and the Divine. Here insights and information can be directly accessed that would not be possible in a state of Consciousness. On this plane, imagery therapy can quickly and easily facilitate gaining insight, wisdom, and shifts in a person and then shift those aspects often in minutes. This advanced use of imagery and visualization integrates all of the five senses and is interactive with the therapist. The hallmark of this approach is that everything comes from the client, and the therapist merely elicits the client's shifts and insights. It is therefore an integration of classical psychotherapy and experiential forms of therapy. Rev. Jakob is fully trained and has integrated many forms of image therapy, such as Interactive Guided Imagery, Mindscape (or Silva Method), with hypnotherapy and parts work to provide the most effective form of this therapy.

JAKOB MERCHANT

Generative Therapy

From the Unmanifest, the infinite potential through the archetypal layers of the subconscious, infinite solutions to any situation can be manifested. Generative therapy focuses on bringing this potential into the experiential reality of a person. Utilizing various hypnotic and trance work, this form of therapy includes creating a positive state of Consciousness, or "coach state," in which a person can process anything that arises in Consciousness due to being deeply rooted in choiceless awareness. Further therapy focuses on being in a solution-centered state of Consciousness, developing steps from the Unmanifest toward any goal, working with internalizing role models and utilizing them for one's own hero's journey. It is summarized under the lotus principle that everything in one's life can be utilized for the growth of the client and hence sub-serves the client's highest good. Rev. Jakob studied this form of therapy for many years, training with Stephen Gilligan in person and through his books and other recordings on a daily basis.

Ayurvedic Health Counseling

Ayurveda is one of the oldest healing systems in the world. It is a holistic system that includes treatment via the physical, mental, emotional, energetic, spiritual, and environmental aspects of a human being. At the Health and Healing Clinic the main application of Ayurveda is in lifestyle counseling, as well as how lifestyle can be changed to facilitate healing.

Ayurvedic therapy includes nutrition, herbs, and yoga, meditation as well as working with sacred spiritual texts. The Health and Healing Clinic integrates all of them and individualizes them to each client's needs. Rev. Jakob Merchant is an Ayurvedic Health Counselor receiving the majority of his training from the California College of Ayurveda.

About the Author

Here are some excerpts from Rev. Jakob's personal experiences as they relate to the principles covered in this book. They are not in linear or chronological order but instead organized according to the spiritual principles of this book:

The One Thing You Must Know About the Author:

I am Love's idiot. All good things have come from the grace of Love; nothing from me.

My life has been committed to Love ever since I can remember. This Love may have taken different forms at different ages, but it always was all-important. In my youth, questions of Love took a personal form, then a spiritual one, and then a transcendental one. Love changed form over the years, starting with my mother to women to the Light that shines from all that exists and dwells within everyone.

Illumination, or this Light that is only Love, has been my central awareness and focus for most of this life. My experiences throughout childhood were natural but not intellectually understood. It was only with the help of Dr. David R. Hawkins that I understood and recontextualized this Light of Love as the Divine within, the Purusha.

Life provides in every moment the maximum opportunity for one's spiritual evolution and the direct experience of Love. One need only step back and allow it. Instead of looking elsewhere, maximum spiritual growth is guaranteed by looking at what is. This is for me also the case today. I spent most of my life focused on transcendental experiences; however, I learned that in order to evolve spiritually, the integration with life is necessary. I

JAKOB MERCHANT

still work on this today, along with my kids and wife, as we help others in their process.

Surrender became a central focus of my spiritual journey when I met Dr. Hawkins. However, later I realized that my whole life has been a form of surrender where the journey was to realize that everything is an expression of the Divine, and surrender merely meant to surrender to that.

Spiritual progress is forever ongoing. There is no endpoint. Some have the notion or belief that there is an endpoint to spiritual evolution, but while the state may be complete, there is also the grace to continue on. Infinite Love is infinite and hence whatever awareness and understanding may exist, it is always the beginning. There is the flow of life, however the backdrop of Love remains.

My physical life is now dedicated to being a servant of the Lord of Love, serving those that, seek to deepen the experience of Love, deepen their spirituality, and be the Light.

If my life is ever to be summarized in one sentence, I hope it will be:

"Love is all, Love is all that exists."

Humility

Humility is the end of believing one's experience is reality. Within this radical openness anything can be revealed. This facilitates spiritual progress because spiritual teachings now have the space to become experiential.

When practicing the Course in Miracles, for example, I was walking in the University of Salzburg and a white Light began to shine forth from everything. All the walls, stairs, wood, and people were now suffused by this Light that was only Love. Similar experiences would occur at different times, most noticeably in the subway in Paris, where the Light of Love shined forth from the graffiti in the subways, teaching me that Love can be experienced in everything, no matter what form it may initially appear.

It is the nature of the "I" to believe in one's reality. The "I" naturally assumes that whatever is experienced is reality; humility allows one to let go of this illusion and open to greater realities than the limited "I" has previously experienced.

In high school, a friend of mine invited me to meet Lama Ole Nydahl, who was giving a talk in Passau Germany. I was captivated not only by the spiritual teachings Lama Ole offered but by the humility and radical honesty he had to share. People began to line up, and somebody invited me to join them. As it was my turn, I received the blessing from what I found out later was the relics of all of the sixteen Karmapas; without knowing, I was initiated into Buddhism.

During the next few days, my reality radically began to alter. One spiritual experience I occurred happened during my lunchbreak. Whenever I put a French fry into my mouth, it exploded into an experience of bliss and I became, for a moment, the whole universe. When finding myself back into my body, I repeated this several times. My third eye began to open, and I started to experience reality not through my physical eyes but from a different domain.

I began practicing the sixteenth Karmapa meditation that would lead often into an experience of a golden light that is only Love. At other times, I practiced loving eyes meditation for hours every day. This transformed the world and allowed for a glow of Love to shine forth from people and also objects. I began to fall in love with whatever was in front of me, like the heater that I was sitting in front of during meditations. After practicing the meditation, I would be in Love with the heater as much as one can be in Love with anything.

JAKOB MERCHANT

Attending many retreats, I took in what was shared without any reservation. I radically practiced what was taught, often through the middle of the night for hours on end. This was the case because humility allowed me to be taught. I was not clinging to my own reality of experiencing, which in turn created the space for a higher reality.

Consistency and Unconditional Practice

The single most important factor in my spiritual evolution has been a wholeheartedness and 110 percent dedication and commitment. This led in my applying a spiritual principle, or practice, to the exclusion of anything else. Whatever spiritual practice it was, it was applied and practiced without holding back. Because wholeheartedness directly removes everything that one holds on in form, the formless reveals itself effortlessly.

In the beginning, spiritual practice was practiced over longer periods of time, until the experience of the spiritual practice manifested and became part of life. For example, in the beginning of practicing the Course in Miracles, it may have been weeks of consistent unconditional practice until the practice became experientially reality. This required practicing one lesson for about six months, partially because exceptions were being made. As those exceptions ceased, the lessons' essence shined forth. Eventually, the practice times became shorter, often to the point where many experiences could be connected more consistently in days or even minutes. However, no lesson was bypassed, and each was practiced until it became experiential reality.

With that, scrupulosity of spiritual practices arose. When needed, spiritual practice would be used to enter specific states of Consciousness, while at other times consciously skipped so that it was possible to function in the world. When in college, for example, I required a specific linear focus for finals, so meditation practices stopped. On the other hand, when somebody would come to visit, I practiced the Buddhist loving eyes so that this person would only feel loved, while I would be in love with whoever showed up.

A spiritual practice that required ten minutes of meditation every full hour made it necessary to stop the car when driving to longer-distance places and to stop writing an exam in the middle, as spiritual work was prioritized over everything else. One moment that particularly stands out in my mind occurred when my girlfriend at that time was watching a television show while I relentlessly practiced the spiritual practice of that particular time. I was not aware of what she watched on television, nor could I recollect any part of it. All of my attention and awareness was completely absorbed inside in the spiritual practice despite the fact that she sat next to me in front of the television. Form had become irrelevant.

One mistake I made at this time happened because spiritual experiences became a natural and daily occurrence, and I experienced a sense of complacency. Because spiritual states could be experienced seemingly "at will," I felt it was all right to just have some "fun with life" and revisit the topic later, whenever needed. It took a long period of time until I realized that this was in and of itself a defense mechanism of the "I." The only way out was the reaffirmation of surrendering to Love and thereby being the manifestation of God's will with no personal gain of any kind. Spiritual practice needed to be practiced at all times, all circumstances, and with no exceptions, no matter what the consequence because it is done for the Divine and not the individual self.

Applying a spiritual principle or teaching at all times and above all else is of more importance to spiritual progress than anything else. This 110 percent dedication always has been part of my life and all progress is attributed to it. It is summarized by the sacred Indian saying that one needs to "want God as much as the drowning man wants air[5]." This is not only true for every area of life but especially for having a living spirituality. With the ferociousness of purpose and unconditional practice, spiritual progress becomes effortless.

---

5 Traditionally attributed to the Upanishads, the sacred texts of India.

Surrender and The Personal Will

Surrender would mean many different things to me over the years. This would depend on my own identification at that time. While surrendering the world, I would spend about one year in deep meditation and contemplation removed from the rest of the world in a self-designed semi monastic setting.

Not knowing intellectually what surrender meant, I was merely praying "Lord, surrender everything as it arises for me." I would make sure that every single moment I was holding this intention. Every single thought was replaced with this prayer, and eventually this white light would begin to shine forth from within and surround me. It is the surrendered state that replaces the individual self.

The servanthood of surrender allows one to go through anything, eventually realizing one is Consciousness and not subject to what arises. I was driving in a car when all of form faded away. Just as the higher states of Consciousness are formless, illumined, and with no content, so are the lowest states of Consciousness. The "I" experienced itself beyond a body, beyond a mind, in a formless state of hopelessness and anguish. In this state, the prayer arose invoking Divinity and I realized that the anguish was resistance to eternal hopelessness. I could either resist the state of hopelessness forever and experience the anguish on top of it, or accept hopelessness with no end. In this moment, arose "For Thee O Lord do I surrender and remain in eternal hopelessness." Because my life is not really mine but that of the Lord's, anything that I am asked I do with no restraints or conditions. Because there was no looking for personal gain or concern for my person, I merely did what I was asked as a servant of the Lord. This complete and total surrender then disappeared this experience, and I was back in the car. While the experience was outside of time, not even a few seconds of earthly time had passed. With complete and total surrender, this state had disappeared. Out of this experience, I retained a knowingness that will carry me through whatever else may be. If we do something for ourselves, there is only so far we can go; if we do it for the Love, there is no limit how far we can go. This experience of surrender allowed me the certainty that whatever arises in Consciousness is irrelevant; a servant of the Lord does not have an aversion to anything; he is protected by his complete surrender.

Love is all that Exists

Love is all that exists. My life has been dedicated and centered around Love and the spiritual questions of Love. Can Love be gained or lost? Can form be manipulated so one can experience more of it? Is Love the ultimate reality?

When I was a child, my mother went back to work, an event that triggered the question of whether Love can be lost. Years passed by, as I looked for Love in different places, people, and activities. I eventually realized that Love is not something to be found or bargained with. It is nothing to be gained or achieved, but merely surrendered to. It is available in any moment; nothing is holding it back but the illusionary belief that it would be otherwise.

One of the biggest lessons I learned around Love was centered around the clouds that were seemingly hiding it. Among them, abandonment, the absence of God's Love as a great emptiness was a central theme. After watching a movie on black holes, nightmares occurred for years in which I would dream to be sucked back into a place that is devoid of everything, especially devoid of Love. Being born to transcend the belief system that the Void or great emptiness is the ultimate reality, a journey of a lifetime began when my mother went back to work. Eventually, the feeling of abandonment was replaced with a Love that was the background of existence. It would be almost twenty-five years later when I realized Love's reality beyond the coming and goings of form.

JAKOB MERCHANT

Similar to my nightmares as a child, Buddhism led me into that great emptiness as a teenager. Many spiritual experiences occurred over the years that I practiced Buddhism. Illumination, the experience of an inner light eventually became a regular occurrence. However, there was this notion or belief that illumination was not the ultimate reality and must be negated as a distraction that had been created by the mind. A common Buddhist belief, it led me repeatedly into a space that is devoid of everything through meditation, only at that point it happened consciously. This space is best described as a space that has no content of any kind but at the same time is the absence of Love. Returning repeatedly into this space in meditation over the course of months, the question, Is this it?, arose. Is this the end of the spiritual journey? Feeling incomplete, a shift between me and Buddhism began to take place.

This eventually led to Dr. David R. Hawkins. However, even after years of transformation and working with his teachings, a subconscious alignment with negation remained. This only changed when Dr. Hawkins looked into my eyes and said, that I could stay in the Void forever. In that moment, the secret allegiance to the pathway of negation and its seemingly ultimate reality was broken. It was truly in the grace of Love that the trap of my own making was finally broken. I was free to embrace Love.

Perhaps the most important spiritual lesson learned in this lifetime has been the understanding that there is nothing beyond Love–that Love is the ultimate reality and that every experience of Love, no matter how minuscule, is already a glimpse of the Divine. To experience Love is to experience the Divine, to be Love is to be the Divine.

I remember sitting at the deathbed of Dr. David R. Hawkins. As I sat down and he had asked how can I help you today, the answer that came from the depth of this heart was, "I only want to be like you." The absolute Infinite Love. This commitment I renew every day, knowing that one day I will be able to share the gift of Love that was given to me in that moment. The purpose of this life is to Love and help others to be that Love. When the mind distracts us from that Love, it is spiritual work to remember that Love.

With the help of meditation and contemplation, a tendency of childhood began to settle in which was to effortlessly fall in Love with almost anyone. Out of that, I learned that the blocks to experience Love were not absolute conditions on the outside but merely something the mind had created, a distraction, an illusion to the direct experience that is always present. In any given moment, one can go beyond the positions of the mind into the Love that lays beyond them.

The purpose of this incarnation is to be Love, teaching others how to Love by loving them and holding that loving space for them along their own journey. Love is the beginning and the end of all spirituality. It is the very mechanism of what it means to be spiritual and alive. This is what our place, our courses and books are based on. The understanding that there is nothing more important than Love and the need to be reminded of that. Instead of getting lost in the business of life, one gets lost in Love. Instead of focusing on many spiritual teachings, practices, or scriptures, one focuses on the one that is the essence of them all. One needs not an advanced teacher to find Love, but merely a willingness to say yes to that Love in every moment. One needs not advanced texts or secret scriptures. Saying yes to Love in the moment, surrendering to Love in the moment, is not only sufficient but the highest form of spirituality.

At the end, when people may ask who is this Rev. Jakob?, the truth is that he is an idiot. However, he is Love's idiot, knowing that all good things that came into his life and that are freely given to others are by the grace of Love and left on his own devices there would be no Love.

JAKOB MERCHANT

Surrender to Love

Surrender to Love is giving one's self to the very source of one's being. It is out of such an unrestricted love for Love that one forgoes the individual self.

Many years ago around Christmas, I was in bed listening to a speaker. In this space, arose out of nowhere the absolute knowingness that my life no longer belonged to me and that it was over as I knew it. Coming out of this state, I rewound the tape to hear what was said in that moment when this experience happened. He quoted a book from a spiritual teacher living in Sedona, Arizona. Curious about what happened, I ordered the book and later videos of Dr. David R. Hawkins.

A year passed by, and in studying the writings and videos of Dr. Hawkins, the same absolute knowingness arose in me; the knowingness to give my life completely to the Lord. I was on my way to give my life to the Divine; no reservations, no conditions, nothing to hold for myself and, most importantly, nothing to get out of it. Just as the servants of God would stand before Jesus, Krishna or Buddha, I would go to Sedona and reaffirm: Anything you want Lord.

With this intention to give my life entirely and without reservation to the Lord, the Divine, I walked up the stairs and sat down. At that moment the whole world faded away; all of form faded away, and I was suffused by this golden light that was only Love, was the only thing that existed. It was what I gave my life to. I surrendered to Love.

This experience of inner Light sometimes rose daily when I was growing up. Now, however, its meaning and significance had been altered. When the "I" dissolves, it is replaced by this light, which is only Love. Growing up, there were times I resisted it, but now I had learned to surrender and dissolve into it.

Many years of my youth were spent in reflection, contemplation, and studying as well as practicing what later could be called the Truth of Love. I tried to manipulate the occurrence of spiritual experiences via certain behaviors and practices, expecting some reward for this form of manipulation. All the studies and training, the master's degree and therapy training, as well as daily spiritual practices in all of the world religions, meant little compared to the realization that Love already is, and we merely surrender to it.

The "I" and Its Identifications: Thoughts and Mentalization

At a five-day retreat, surrender was practiced continuously without exception. Not only during formal sitting meditations but also during walking, eating—every moment had one sustained intention of continuous surrender. The main focus was within the mind, thoughts, and thinkingness to be surrendered.

On one of the five days, many different thought patterns and questions arose. Most prominently was the question, "How do I surrender?" Meanwhile, there was an ongoing prayer: "Lord surrender for me everything as it arises." I didn't need to know how to surrender as I merely asked the Divine to do so on my behalf.

Eventually thoughts became less and less, and the very question of how to surrender disappeared. It was only then that I realized there was an accumulated energy that had expressed itself in the form of this question. Throughout the days of meditation, this energy was already surrendering and dissipating. When it was completely gone, the question on how to surrender—its form or expression—was as well. The question had been answered not by receiving an intellectual answer but by the question itself disappearing. In this way, it allowed for Truth to stand in its place.

The days and continuous practice continued and for a split second the mind became silent and bliss ensued. Caught off guard as my focus was on continuous surrender, thoughts rushed back in.

After a while I recommitted to the spiritual practice of surrendering everything as it arose, disregarding what had happened, and in that moment silent bliss ensued again. This time it lasted for a longer time, but even after a few seconds, maybe a minute, thoughts came rushing back in. I realized my interest toward that state of Consciousness over my devotion to my spiritual practice "no matter what"; after that realization I recommitted to the practice, disregarding what had happened.

Now the state came on more permanently, however I realized a slight and subtle attraction to the silent and bliss; in that moment that there was this attraction, and with it an aversion to thought, the silent bliss went away yet again with thoughts reappearing. I realized that it was this attraction to the silent state of Consciousness and the very aversion to thoughts that was holding me in place. My spiritual pathway always has been to become a complete servant of the Lord with no personal gain involved for the self or "I." With this, just like a warrior walking into battle, I committed to the spiritual practice of surrender over bliss, over silence, over anything else. Even if there would be thinkingness forever, I would gladly accept it for the Lord had chosen it (not the "I").

In this moment, without resistance to thought or attractions to silence, silent bliss ensued and remained throughout the night. In this silence arose a knowingness that I could remain in this context of permanent retreat and silent bliss indefinitely. However, it would be only by returning into the world that further spiritual progress could happen. When returning to the world, thoughts would come back and arise, however a shift in relationship to thoughts and thinkingness had happened. They were no longer my thoughts. The "I" was no longer identified as thoughts and the paradigm called mind. Continuous surrender of thought and mentalization led to de-identification of the "I" as mind.

The "I" and Its Identifications: Sense of Doer-Ship[6]

At another retreat, I was sitting and meditating and praying: " Lord, show me how to surrender." In that moment, I experienced a sudden urge to get up from meditation. As I was walking down the hallway, I witnessed my hand coming up and combing through my hair. However, what was radically different was that I hadn't actually done it. I was witnessing the hand moving by itself. I had discovered a feeling or a sense that would feel "I am doing"; which was absent in that moment. Once I discovered this very subtle sense, I devoted every second of the next several months to its dissolution. The recognizing of this sense or feeling was the answer to my prayers. From that moment forward I would focus continuously and without exception on that feeling and surrender it. I would also hold the intention of negating it, often using the mantra, "There is no doer behind the deeds." Eventually the feeling of doer-ship dropped away as well as any notion or experience of the "I" as the doer of actions. From then on, the body interacted with the world exactly as before but with no inherent feeling of "I" in its actions.

The "I" and its Identifications: Witnessing and Attention

At yet another retreat I was again praying "Lord, show me how to surrender." This time, my focus and awareness were drawn to the quality of paying attention. In spiritual work, one utilizes the quality of paying attention for spiritual progress and is often referred to as "one pointedness of mind." However, this time the knowingness arose to surrender focusing itself. Just as before emotions, thinkingness, or the sense of doership, it became clear that I needed to surrender the quality of focusing. Over a period of hours of ongoing meditation, nothing seemed to happen, and yet the overall in

---

6 The belief of being the doer of one's actions. A common illusion, the "I" claims power over actions, deeds or movements of the body

tention of surrendering that which focuses continued until focusing itself became autonomous with no "I" involved with it. Just as before, whatever is surrendered will be discovered to be an autonomous quality of Divinity without any causal or identifiable "I." From this moment, the "I" was Consciousness and awareness but no longer the one to focus or pay attention. Focusing happened by itself from then on.

Spiritual Practices and Applications

Spiritual Community

Over the years, I have encountered many spiritual communities as I immersed myself with the teacher or teaching of different traditions. Many of them have had their own style or culture. All of them have had expectations of what is appropriate and spiritual, and each followed an interpretation of their teachings.

Some communities of which I had been a part showed a high level of spiritual maturity, tolerance, and compassion. All of them understood that meditation and one's inner spiritual work was most important. Their hallmark, however, was an "unconditional support" of one's spiritual journey as well as a lack of pride about themselves, thereby offering an unconditional loving context that had no requirements.

Other spiritual communities taught me what a spiritual community needs, simply by their lack of these qualities. The lack of unconditional Love and compassion as well as high forms of rigidity and implicit judgment became a hindrance to the group and its members' spiritual evolution. This was mainly based on the pride that the group possessed concerning itself and its teacher. One hallmark of the dysfunctional spiritual group is that its members are enamored with themselves and thereby pride themselves on being "better than," which in itself prevents unconditional loving support. Thanks to these insights, I decided it was best to create a spiritual community that spans denominations, creeds, and belief systems, and provides the best possible circumstances for spiritual evolution. While I was never interested in being part of any particular spiritual group, I did realize that one becomes the average of the people one is aligned with and hence the dictum to keep Love's company. Out of this formed Communion with Love, a community dedicated to Love and the pathway of the heart irrespective of belief.

Spiritual Counseling

Perhaps the most significant support I encountered along my spiritual journey was derived from spiritual counseling. I found over the years that there is nothing more valuable than receiving teaching, support, and guidance in an unconditional loving space. What makes spiritual counseling different is that it is uniquely tailored to the individual. One time, for example, I had a question. Two other people had already asked the very same question before me. I hesitated since the question had already been answered. Nevertheless, I asked the question and the answer I received was totally different from what the teacher had shared minutes prior. It was not the answer, but my answer.

Another powerful aspect of spiritual counseling that I encountered is that loving awareness of another being shines the Light of Love on to a person's perception. Most often just the sharing in an unconditional loving context is sufficient to produce a person's transformation. This sharing with another being is a time-honored practice in all traditions. Whether actual advice is given in addition to that is secondary to the fact that awareness and Love are transformational. This is because with awareness and Love, a person is seen and loved for what they are and thereby taught to Love by loving them. I encountered this with advanced spiritual teachers as much as with people who were seemingly new to the spiritual journey. Their commitment to be loving and present was what facilitated the spiritual journey.

JAKOB MERCHANT

Over the years, I also learned that while a spiritual journey has commonalities, it is inherently unique to each individual. One's path to Love is based on one's unique background, culture, and belief systems. Only spiritual counseling can account for individuality by traveling this pathway of Love together.

Be to Others What You Want for Yourself

The Divine transmission of Love is available at all places and circumstances but is most palpable around someone who is open to be that Love to others. To focus on a teacher or teaching is to connect to them; meditation, worship and contemplation invites understanding, insights, and unseen support into one's life. While beneficial, it is not necessary to physically meet a teacher in order to receive the blessings of Love.

The best way to learn anything is to be what one aspires for others. Hence, I encourage you to take any part of this work without restrictions and share it with others. No written permission to share any of the work in any format is required if cited correctly and the work itself has not been altered to ensure its original meaning. I further encourage you to connect any aspect of these principles with your own insights and experiences because within these experiences lies the power for transformation.

Please use "Work cited without alteration" by Rev. Jakob Merchant.

Find more information at

www.jakobmerchant.com/freelyhaveyourecieved

Gifts of Love

Love has intersected with you via this book. If you like to deepen this relationship with Love, we offer you a free guided meditation that integrates the principles outlined in this book.

You can access the meditation here:

www.communionwithlove.com/10principlesgift

If you have purchased the printed version of this book, we would like to gift you the digital version.

Visit:

www.communionwithlove.com/10principles-to-a-living-spirituality

to receive your free copy.

The online course 10 days to a Living Spirituality as well as the book and meditation bundle in the Communion with Love store both include a copy of 10 Principles to a Living Spirituality. Because you already purchased the book, use the coupon code **"gifts of love"** for a 10% discount on both the online course and the book bundle.

Professional Training - Highlights

» **Grand Canyon University**

Phoenix, Arizona
Master of Science in Professional Counseling

» **Ayurveda College of California**

Nevada City, California
Ayurvedic Health Counselor

» **One Spirit Learning Alliance**

New York, New York
InterSpiritual Counselor
Interfaith minister

» **Milton H. Erickson Institute**

Mastery Training in Ericksonian
Brief Hypnotic Psychotherapy
Individual and group Supervision
Evolution of Psychotherapy
Mastery in Ericksonian Brief Therapy

» **Fundamental Training Center for Mindfulness in Medicine, Health Care, Society**

Systemic Trance Work: A Process For Sustainable Creativity

» **Judith Schafman**

Gestalt therapy and Dream work (individual supervision)

» **Internal Family Systems Therapy**

Internal Family Systems (IFS) for Trauma, Anxiety, Depression, Addiction & More

» **International Bodytalk Association**

  Advanced Bodytalk Courses
  Parama Bodytalk
  Mindscape

» **Tara Brach**

  Radical Self-Acceptance: Healing Shame and Fear in Clinical Practice

» **Kripalu Center for Yoga and Health (Frank Jude Boccio)**

  Mindfulness Yoga Teacher training

» **Yoga Zentrum Passau**

  Yoga teacher training

Memberships and Professional Associations

» Spiritual Directors International

» American Society of Clinical Hypnosis

» One Spirit Learning Alliance

» International Bodytalk Association

» Academy for Guided Imagery

» International Association of Yoga Therapists

» American Counseling Association

Licensures

» Interfaith Minister Yoga Instructor

» Advanced Certified Bodytalk Practioner

» Spiritual Director

» InterSpiritual Counselor

» Master in Professional Counseling

» Ayurvedic Health Counselor

Extended Acknowledgements

This work and especially the book would have not been possible without the infinite contributions of many people. This list is a short glimpse of this grace of Love. The wall of gratitude extends to people that have been a blessing in my life overall.

- » **Peter Schaefer:** For being the rock

- » **Melanie Gierlinger:** Being family

- » **Keith Wong:** Bringing fun into our lives

- » **Mary C. Ransdell:** Your love

- » **Angela Brechmann:** Being our spiritual family

- » **Fran Grace:** For your unconditional support

- » **Mary Piotrowski:** For teaching me to be Love's messenger

- » **Daniel Harner:** Being the best brother anyone can have

- » **Joshua Ludeman:** Helping us to start the Sedona Surrender Retreat House

- » **Walter Commons:** For being a friend

- » **Laura Macdonagh:** For your love

- » **Dermot Macdonagh:** For your honesty and friendship

- » **Misun Oh:** For answering the call

- » **Kira Sapach:** Being a Light in my life

- » **Giuseppe Medlin:** For integrating body, heart and spirituality

- » **Ryan McGinty:** For being my band of brothers

- » **Verena Schwarzbauer:** For the joy of childhood

JAKOB MERCHANT

Wall of Gratitude - The Grace of Love in Rev. Jakob's Life

John Gluch	Jazz du Pasquier	Anni Loderbauer
Kausee Raman	Julie Williams	Bob Rutter
Carol Davies	Carli Anderson	Bobbie Sumner
Stipo Sentic	Paul C Anderson	Brian Atkins
Eric & Stephanie	Francois du Pasquier	Brian Trent
Berger	Mark Morris	Cal Regula
Melanie Buzek	Sybille Kitzberger	Caleb Ludeman
Rob McMullen	Ernst Gierlinger	Carol Phelps
Donna Valentine	St. Anthony of	Cheryl Davis
Pir Zia Inayat-Kahn	Cottonwood	Christian
Judy Field	Johanna Seidl	Schwarzbauer
Sonia Martin	William Dopson	Christy Taylor
Debra Henry	Eddie Craig	Claudia
Darren Dickinson	David Seifert	Getzendorfer
Ecker Family	Flor Mazeda	Daniel Heindl
Karl Wisemann	Jordan Keenan	Darren J. Hardy
Aimee Phoenix	Andrea Western	Dr. Kahlenbach
Carmen Straight	Carina Woess	Elizabeth Chetham
Adam Contos	Alois Woess	Elke Gierlinger

Michel B. Beckwith

Christopher O'Hare

Michael Parrott

Maria Demolder

Lauren Malmgren

Christina Mantel

Donna Hollman

Nancy Pharr

Dawn Phillips Morris

Susan Cloutier

Pam Malmgren

Jim Wilkins

Claudette Monica

Powell

William Frazier

Bernhard Rauoecker

Holger Woess

John Siler

Laura Stuve

Christian Maier

Helene Lorenz

Tatiana Lazdins

Bernhard Wundsam

Markus Maier

Lama Ole Nydahl

Kurt Kagerer

Christopher Brouwer

Ernestine Woess

Arvind Kumar

Don Western

Vilnis Muiznieks

Sherry Ritley

Warren Allabastro

Michele Paz Solden

Jack Canfield

Johann "Hans"

Gierlinger

Johannes Gierlinger

John Veltheim

Kathy and Larry

Jaeckel

Kisah Dan Chin

Kobit Beaver

Kurt Krammer

Leslie Gleatches

Maja Martinuc

Manne Britz

Mark Lazarakis

Max and Monika

Rauocker

Otto Gierlinger

Rita & Annabella

Kumar

Russ Venable

Sarah Mowdy

Scott Phelps

Sharon Moyer

Don & Gisela

Mcdonagh

Darlene Leslie Denis

Sylvia Muiznieks

Daniel Lorenz

Alison Etter

Pumberger family

Peter Pumberger

Mayrhofer Family

Christian Birngruber

Tim Hall

Andrew Facca

Candice A. Torresdal

Johanna Mocsa

Dalida Amalean

Ann O'Neil

David Wallace

Dannielle Richards

Xena Olsen

Dan Denis

You

Steffen Berlenbach

Sherri Sharkins

Malcon Taylor

Christoph Kurzboeck

Donna Robinson

Arthur Wundsam

Beth Drewett

Beth Drewett

Janet Galipo

Hermina Munnsad

Michelle Warner

Joyce Lichenstein

Ron Foster

Stefan Dobretsberger

Trevor Triano

Stephen Gilligan

Ullricke Dobretsberger

Verena Schwarzbauer

Vicky and Jack Jenkins

Linda Foshie

William Taylor

Markus Freund

Lauren Brim

Michel Frances O'Hare

Ann O'Neil

Chantal Matthews

Experiences with Rev. Jakob

"Jakob Merchant is one of those rare people who fill a substantial place in my heart of hearts without seeming to be there at all. He represents Infinite Love and Devotion, and when I feel the need to entrain with that deep untarnished space within, he is there. When I am not sure what step to take next, he is there. When there is confusion and doubt, he is there—always with the perfect exercise, the right meditation, the overarching perspective. Jakob's insight, wisdom, and loving space have made a palpable difference in my life. The book you are holding in your hands will prove invaluable to set you on a more direct course to the truth of the Love you are."

[ALISON ETTER OF NELSON, BRITISH COLUMBIA]

"10 Principles to a Living Spirituality is a concise guide of meaningful steps for one's spiritual practice. Its simplicity, honesty and heartfelt direction is foundational for getting one on track towards an unconditionally loving life in the Presence of Love as all that exists. Reverend Jakob Merchant's writings, spiritual guidance, and spiritual leadership have been instrumental for me in Living Spirituality today and every day."

[VIRGINIA SCHLITT OF AUSTIN, TEXAS]

"This book condenses much of what I've learned from various teachings and experiences on my own spiritual journey, while also providing fresh drops of wisdom. I think it holds the potential to save the spiritual aspirant much time by outlining and clarifying core spiritual principles. It also emphasizes surrendering to Love at a profound depth that I aspire to in my own life."

[WALTER COMMONS OF SEDONA, ARIZONA]

"Rev. Jakob Merchant has distilled the vital steps along the path leading to enhanced spirituality and put it in a format that's easy to keep handy for the purpose of reading often. These enlightening tenets bear repetition. Very uplifting! A book I want to keep on my nightstand."
[BARBARA THOMSON OF SEDONA, ARIZONA]

"Selecting any one of the principles or practices outlined in this book and applying it, living it, fixating on it, consistently, without exception, no matter what, can take you the whole way Home to the realization of the Highest Truth. Rev. Jakob has an innate capacity and a rigorous willingness to adhere to these principles and practices in his own life, ergo the presence of the conviction behind his work is the real deal. When I look into his eyes, which look back at me with raw Love (from Above he always reminds me), I witness my whole body soften, the stress and resistance I didn't even know the depth of which I may have been holding at the time, literally dissipates and, as I surrender to that inner peace, within seconds, a blast of Power bursts open my heart, repeatedly. This sounds like an unusual phenomenon; it is my fortunate reality. May this fortune come upon you too. "
[ROMY ALEXANDRA OF SEDONA, ARIZONA]

"2014년 제이콥을 처음 만났던 날을 기억한다. 서로 알지 못하는 상태에서 우리는 한동안 서로의 눈을 바라보고 있었다. 그 순간을 말로 표현하려 하면 무언가 핵심이 빠진 느낌이다. 그나마 가장 적합한 표현은 온전한 현존의 경험이었다는 것이다. 세도나로 이사온 지 2년 반, 그 시간을 제이콥을 빼고 말할 순 없다. 제이콥 집에서 매일 저녁 진행되는 Devotional Service, 매주 일요일 진행되는 Surrender Group, 그리고 정기적으로 진행되는 Workshop 과 Retreat. 제이콥과 그의 가족의 삶은 말 그대로 헌신이고 타인에 대한 봉사였다. 작은 자아를 온전히 내려놓지 못한 존재라면 감히 해낼 수 없는 일이다. 세도나에서의 새로운 삶이 나의 오래된 더미들을 끌어올릴 때면, 나는 서렌더하우스로 향하곤 했다. 나 혼자서는 도저히 감당이 안 되던 그 더미가 서렌더하우스에서 하루 이틀 머무는 동안 자연스레 내맡겨지는 경험을 얼마나 많이 했는지 모른다. 매번 워크샵과 리트릿 또한 언제나 조금씩 에고가 가벼워지는 시간이었다. 그러나 제이콥은 단 한번도 자기를 내세우거나 크레딧을 주장한 적이 없었다. 그저 무한한 신의 은총이 제이콥을 통해 일하도록 스스로를 신의 종의 자리에 두는 것, 그게 제이콥이 하는 전부였다. 세도나에 사는 2년 동안 나의 삶은 엄청나게 변했고(내적, 외적 모두) 그 변화에는 항상 제이콥의 도움이 있었다.

"I remember the day I first met Jakob in 2014. Without knowing each other, we looked into each other's eyes for a while. If I try to express that moment in words, something is missing. The closest expression might be the experience of being fully present. Now two and a half years since I moved to Sedona, my life would not be the same without Jakob. My life has become more devotional thanks to the services Jakob provides. Devotional Service are offered every evening, Surrender Group every Sunday, and Workshops or Retreats on a regular basis at Jakob's house. Jakob and his family's life is literally a devotion to God and a service to others. If you can't surrender the little self, you can't do this. When my new life in Sedona pulled up some old stacks, I used to go to Surrender house on retreat. I could not have managed these stacks alone, but it was made possible when I stayed at Surrender House. Also, after each workshop or retreat, things were always a little bit lighter. Jakob never tried to claim credit for my experiences. Jakob simply put himself in the position of a servant of God so that the Infinite Grace of God could work through him. For two years in Sedona, my life has changed tremendously (both internally and externally), and these changes have always been thanks to Jakob's help. "

[MISUN OH OF SEDONA, ARIZONA]

"I have been a patient of Jakob's for years. Through his treatments, I have healed areas in my life I did not know needed work. There were issues I had carried around with me through lifetimes. What a relief to be able to let go off all that baggage! Jakob is highly skilled in BodyTalk and extremely accurate in his diagnosis and treatment. He has treated me with honesty, integrity, kindness, and compassion every single time, and his intention has always been to help heal me. I always look forward to my sessions with Jakob!"

[DALIDA OF CHARLOTTE, NORTH CAROLINA]

"This short but dense book is a collaboration of the highest spiritual truths and practices that alone can accomplish the seemingly impossible. Jakob is uniquely matched to share these truths as he lives and lovingly practices them continuously. Finally, these highest of principles are condensed for easy review and reference.

My work with Jakob has been such a blessing. As I look back I see the paradigm I was living, the level of Consciousness I was identified with, and I have to laugh a little. Bless my heart. The subtleties in the moment turn into the obvious and profound when seen over time. In Jacob's sessions, one benefits from the intention and level of awareness as well as a Consciousness-based system of identifying and integrating the blockages, past belief systems, and various energy fields that are the perceived obstacles to higher awareness. The bottom line for me is that it makes the Path a lot faster and easier. Thank you, brother. As you always say, Much Love."

[MALCON TAYLOR OF NASHVILLE, TENNESSEE]

"Fabiola and Jakob are Ambassadors of Love and Light and their beautiful Yoga Retreat is the perfect Spiritual home-away-from-home. Trust me, you won't want to stay in a hotel ever again! My heart and soul literally sang at the sublime décor - in fact as soon as I saw the photo of my bed I was sold! :-) Their home is a living dream, with such beautiful soothing colors, textures and spiritual artwork - that I felt my heart melt when-ever I discovered another room. I rented the studio called the 'Yoga Retreat' because I wanted by own private bathroom, but there are other beautiful rooms available (all with lovely names) that were simply romantic! Everything is so clean and inviting that you feel relaxed and comfortable.

This is a very healing environment. I am forever enriched by the experience of celebrating my birthday in view of the exquisite Sedona landscape that surrounds their property. It was wonderful to sit on their lovely furnished patio and enjoy the delicious continental breakfast their provided, whilst bathed in sun-light. Stones shaped like Guardians looked over me and the incredible Cathedral Rock loomed majestically in the distance. This retreat location is close to stores and incredible vortexes, yet remote enough that you feel you are truly away from it all. The peace here is like a living prayer! Oak Creek river is a short walk way and I loved the neighborhood hikes that Fabiola encourage you to explore. I so enjoyed the yoga session I had with Jakob on top of a cliff before Cathedral Rock. The setting was surreal! I felt so loved and welcomed and their whole family is simply a joy to be around. Yep, whenever I visit Sedona, I am definitely staying here! THANK YOU, Fabiola and Jakob, from my heart to yours, Still smiling, Heather.'"

[HEATHER OF LOS ANGELES, CALIFORNIA]

"Jakob has been an unwavering expression of the Infinite Field of Love since I first met him. Sure, it is easy to express kindness and generosity when we feel like it or when it is deserved. Jakob's commitment goes far beyond sporadic displays of obligatory politeness. Under any circumstance, Jakob yields to Divine Will, an incredible example of what surrender to the Field is, rather than one's own personal wants, seeming needs, or any opposing doubts or thoughts. As the Field often is at odds with what we think is the right attitude or action, this is far more difficult than one would presume. Shoulds and reasoning and everything one has learned may have to be given up, as the Field of Love always serves to the Highest Good and will take us beyond what we already know, as the path is evolutionary. Jakob is a true friend to Devotional Non-duality students from all over the world, serving all as a constant expression of the Infinite Field of Love. He is a living demonstration of the power of surrender. His capacity to surrender everything, including his own life to Divine Will continues to expand my own capacity, for which I am endlessly grateful.

JAKOB MERCHANT

Jakob is your man. Fixing all the physical issues was also awesome, but giving my soul some peace and understanding was incredible. God Bless you Jakob!"

[JANE FROM NUTRITION WITH JANE, NEW JERSEY]

"*This is a book to ponder. Words that can change the way we experience life. Take your time and savor the deep meaning in how this information applies to who you are and who you want to become. This is nurturing food for the soul. The mind, body, and soul can be finally tuned. Let Jakob be your tuning fork. Love it, live it, share it.*"

[KATHY MASTERS-JAECKEL, INTUITIVE COUNSELOR
FOR FORTY YEARS]

JAKOB MERCHANT

Made in the USA
Monee, IL
13 December 2019

As a dear colleague, friend, and fellow spiritual student, he has inspired, lead, and been the very Spirit of patience, devotion, and dedication. I once was blessed with an opportunity to bring Jakob and a few other students who were aligned with devotion, healing, and Love into a clinical setting where we treated extremely difficult conditions. By the presence alone of these sincerely aligned students, the space itself became a healing vessel. Chaos transformed into a divinely orchestrated flow of inspiration, hope, and freedom. Each individual entering the clinic was immersed in an absolute intention to relieve suffering. The Field itself prioritized everything and infused the courage for all who participated to give up attachment to long-term ills, endless suffering, and all that had been in the way of the shift in Consciousness needed to truly heal. Some healed to an extraordinary degree on a physical level, some healed deeply internally; many, I suspect, cannot define what exactly happened, and some have yet to fully integrate the experience. Working with Jakob in a clinical setting was an extraordinary experience in witnessing the field working through us all. Jakob constantly allows the field to work, setting a healing tone that fills the space with the highest potential for healing and a palpable immersion of unconditional lovingness."

[SARAH MOWDY OF SAN FRANCISCO, CALIFORNIA]

"I have no words to say other than my heartfelt thanks and gratitude to what Jakob represents, and to his wife for hosting such a blessed service, meditation, and devotional Enlightenment retreat/workshop! I have always looked forward to these services even though I live in Tucson, three and a half hours away!"

[KISAH DAN CHIN OF TUCSON, ARIZONA]

"You have done so much for me. Thank you is not enough! I believe you came to me and helped me at a time my soul was calling out for additional guidance was no coincidence. For those who stride for spiritual growth,